Materials Design Using Computational Intelligence Techniques

Materials Design
Using Computational
Intelligence Techniques

Shubhabrata Datta

CRC Press
Taylor & Francis Group
Boca Raton   London   New York

CRC Press is an imprint of the
Taylor & Francis Group, an **informa** business

CRC Press
Taylor & Francis Group
6000 Broken Sound Parkway NW, Suite 300
Boca Raton, FL 33487-2742

First issued in paperback 2020

© 2017 by Taylor & Francis Group, LLC
CRC Press is an imprint of Taylor & Francis Group, an Informa business

No claim to original U.S. Government works

ISBN 13: 978-0-367-57433-8 (pbk)
ISBN 13: 978-1-4822-3832-7 (hbk)

Version Date: 20160817

International Standard Book Number-13: 978-1-4822-3832-7 (Hardback)

Visit the Taylor & Francis Web site at
http://www.taylorandfrancis.com

and the CRC Press Web site at
http://www.crcpress.com

Dedicated to my parents and teachers

Contents

List of Figures

List of Software and Web Resources

Here is a list of software packages and web resources on the computational tools used, particularly the computational intelligence-based techniques, viz. artificial neural network, fuzzy logic and genetic algorithm. The list is not at all a comprehensive one. It only includes the software packages and sources used by the author and/or known to the author for their effectiveness.

Software

Artificial Neural Network

- MATLAB® Neural Network Toolbox (Commercial)
- STATISTICA Automated Neural Networks (Commercial)
- BrainMaker, BrainMaker Pro (Commercial)
- NeuroSolutions (Commercial)
- CIlib—Computational Intelligence Library (Free)
- JustNN (Free)

Fuzzy Logic

- MATLAB Fuzzy Logic Toolbox (Commercial)
- Free Fuzzy Logic Library (Free)

Genetic Algorithm

- MATLAB Genetic Algorithm Toolbox (Commercial)
- GeneHunter (Commercial)
- GA in C (Free)
- NSGA II (Free)
- SPGA II (Free)

Web Sources

- A Definition of Soft Computing – adapted from L.A. Zadeh (http://www.soft-computing.de/def.html)
- IEEE Computational Intelligence Society (http://cis.ieee.org/)
- World Federation of Soft Computing (http://www.softcomputing.org/)
- Artificial Intelligence (http://www.dmoz.org/Computers/Artificial_Intelligence/)
- Neural Networks in Materials Science (http://www.msm.cam.ac.uk/phase-trans/abstracts/neural.review.html)
- Kanpur Genetic Algorithms Laboratory – IIT Kanpur (http://www.iitk.ac.in/kangal/index.shtml)
- FuzzyTECH (http://www.fuzzytech.com/)
- Genetic Algorithm Warehouse (http://geneticalgorithms.ai-depot.com/)
- Data Mining, Analytics, Big Data, and Data Science (http://www.kdnuggets.com)

Preface

First, I need to clarify that this book is not meant for developing expertise in computational intelligence (CI) techniques. As its title suggests, it focusses purely on the application of the tools for the purpose of materials design. Does that mean one first has to know about the CI techniques before reading this book, to understand the applications properly? No, absolutely not. All of the tools are adequately described before we go into the case studies, to explain how they can be applied for materials modelling, simulation and optimisation. But those explanations are intended only to give readers sufficient insight to understand the basic mathematics behind the techniques and how they can use the tools for their own purposes, not to make them experts in handling the tools. I have intentionally avoided going into the details of the techniques, because there are many books and plentiful materials on the web dealing with them, written by experts in the field. It is better not to try learning computational tools from a materials engineer. As a materials engineer, and handling these computational tools for nearly two decades, I understand how much one should as a minimum know about these computational tools before starting to work with them.

First you need to identify the tools you wish to use in the materials systems of your interest, and for that you need to know why and how to use them. In this book I have tried to focus on those issues to inspire readers to start using the tools. Yes, there are matters such as using software and so on to handle the tools. I have provided a list for that also, so that readers, if they wish, can start using the tools. But to go beyond what the software and the free downloadable codes provide, one needs to develop one's own code. Readers who are able to do so should start writing their own code, and otherwise collaborate with someone. After all, the approach discussed in this book is entirely interdisciplinary in nature.

This book does, however, contain a detailed description of several case studies on applications of CI in materials systems for solving different types of problems with different approaches and using different tools. This is to make readers understand the promise and prospects of applying the tools. Readers should appreciate the fact that the tools are not made for materials systems only. Materials engineers are just using them to explore and find new materials, and for that purpose even making some modifications in the tools as well. I therefore thought it more important to explain the utility of the tools through case studies, so that readers could formulate their own applications in the areas in which they are working. The case studies given in this book are mostly on alloys, which may discourage researchers working on other materials. By way of explanation, I first wish to mention that I personally work mostly on metallic systems and thus am more conversant about applications in such systems. Needless to say, I have applied the tools in other systems also, and found them no less useful in other systems. But there are other reasons also. The applications of CI techniques are mostly in the direction of alloy design, by other researchers as well. Some applications concern other structural materials too. But in the case of functional materials the applications are few. Researchers working in the computational area of functional materials in most cases prefer *ab initio* methods. That definitely does not mean that application of these techniques in this field is limited in scope. There are immense possibilities; these tools can even be used in a hybridised form with the *ab initio* modelling concepts. If the system you are working in has complexity due to the presence of several predictor or independent variables, if uncertainty is present in any area in the behaviour of the predictor variables or the materials, if there still is imprecise knowledge in some part of system, try these tools. It is enjoyable, I assure you. And I am sure that a certain amount of complexity, uncertainty or imprecision must be present in the materials system of your interest also. An emerging field called 'nano-informatics' has enormous scope for such applications.

Another topic where this book has not made much of a dent is materials processing. Of course there are case studies on process modelling and optimisation, but in all cases design of new materials predominates, as that is the focus of this book. As a result, one important part of materials engineering has taken back seat: extraction or synthesis of materials. This subject may be addressed a separate book.

The love of materials modelling and optimisation is a bit infectious. It grows and grows, and then affects those around you. But we should not forget to take the antidote also. Experimentalists say that what we do does not have any practical implications. It is absolutely true if we do not try to validate our finding experimentally. When we talk about materials design, the development part should follow. Some of the previously published case studies considered here include that experimental aspect also, which may not have mentioned always in this book. Interested readers should consult the complete articles to have a sense of the sequence of CI-based materials design followed by experimental development for validation.

Any computational technique has a mathematical explanation of the entire process, through which the computing is executed. But those mathematical expressions are mostly reduced in this book to improve its readability. As mentioned earlier, the purpose of this book is chiefly to trigger an interest among materials engineers to start working in this field, and I tried to keep it as simple as possible. Books on CI techniques, which are extensively reffered in the chapters, will provide readers with the details of the underlying mathematics. But one thing is certain: the mathematical concepts behind the techniques are not difficult at all.

This book starts with a discussion of the concept of computational materials design. The CI tools are also introduced in Chapter 1. Before going into the details of the tools and their applications in the materials domain, which is the purpose of this book, the conventional tools of computational materials engineering, used for scientific theory–driven and data-driven modelling (statistical), are described briefly in Chapters 2 and 3. Chapter 4 describes artificial neural networks and genetic programming, two CI-based data-driven modelling techniques, with their application in the materials field. Fuzzy rule–based modelling in materials systems is discussed for rules extracted from data in Chapter 5 and for rules generated from imprecise system knowledge in Chapter 6. Chapter 7 introduces the concept of optimisation using evolutionary algorithms and their importance in materials design. There are many examples in which these techniques are used together for designing materials, and such cases are discussed in Chapter 8. Chapter 9 concludes this book with a discussion of some important issues, such as handling uncertainty.

If reading this book stimulates readers to take up one or some of the tools for application, and then gradually develop a passion for them, its purpose will have been achieved.

MATLAB® is a registered trademark of The MathWorks, Inc. For product information, please contact:

The MathWorks, Inc.
3 Apple Hill Drive
Natick, MA 01760-2098 USA
Tel: 508 647 7000
Fax: 508-647-7001
E-mail: info@mathworks.com
Web: www.mathworks.com

Acknowledgements

At the outset I want to express my heartfelt gratitude to my teacher and my PhD supervisor, Prof. Malay K. Banerjee of Malaviya National Institute of Technology, Jaipur, India, for guiding me into this field of work, almost two decades ago. At that time the techniques, mostly popular as soft computing techniques, were in their infancy in terms of their applications in the materials area. But I persisted in the work and continued with the tools. I shall be always grateful to you, sir.

During this course of time several professors and senior colleagues have worked with me directly or encouraged me to pursue this area of computational materials engineering. Prof. Nirupam Chakraborti of the Indian Institute of Technology, Kharagpur, India; Prof. Kalyanmoy Deb of Michigan State University, USA; Prof. Mahdi Mahfouf of University of Sheffield, UK; Prof. H. K. D. H. Bhadeshia of Cambridge University, UK; Prof. Henrik Saxen and Prof. Frank Pettersson of Abo Akademi, Finland; Prof. Seppo Lauhenkilpi of Aalto University, Finland; Dr. Debashish Bhattacharjee of Tata Steel, IJmuiden, the Netherlands; Prof. Krishna Rajan of the University at Buffalo, USA; and Prof. P. P. Chattopadhyay, Prof. Jaya Sil, Prof. N. R. Bandyopadhyay and Prof. S. Chatterjee of the Indian Institute of Engineering Science and Technology, Shibpur, India are just a few names I will never forget to mention. Many thanks for being so helpful and supportive.

Without my co-workers, who have contributed the lions' share in much of the work considered here, I could not have dared to venture writing this book. They are Dr. Partha Dey of the Academy of Technology, Hooghly, India; Dr. Subhas Ganguly of the National Institute of Technology, Raipur, India; Dr. Prasun Das of the Indian Statistical Institute, India; Dr. Arup Nandi of the Central Mechanical Engineering Research Institute, India; Dr. Sandip Ghosh Chowdhury of the National Metallurgical Laboratory, India; Dr. Qian Zhang of the University of Kent, UK; Dr. Itishree Mohanty of Tata Steel, India; Dr. Abhijit Patra of Techno India College of Technology, India; and Prof. Amit Roy Chowdhury, Dr. Debdulal Das, Dr. Swarup Ghosh, Dr. Mallar Ray, Dr. Malay Kundu, Dr. Arijit Sinha and Dr. Swati Dey of the Indian Institute of Engineering Science and Technology, Shibpur, India. My special thanks to Swati for helping me even during the preparation of the manuscript of this book. I am appreciative to my present doctoral students Nashrin Sultana, Subhamita Chakraborty, Titov Banerjee and Tanushree Dutta.

I am grateful to the fine people of CRC Press, particularly Dr. Gagandeep Singh and Laurie Oknowsky, for their constant encouragement, help and guidance. I really put them through a test of patience.

I am greatly indebted to my wife Sangeeta and daughter Meghna for being so understanding during the difficult time of completing this book.

Author

Dr. Shubhabrata Datta, presently a research professor at the School of Mechanical Engineering, SRM University, Kattankulathur, Chennai, India, earned his BE and ME degrees from Calcutta University (B.E. College) and his PhD degree from BESU, Shibpur (presently known as Indian Institute of Engineering Science and Technology), in the field of metallurgical and materials engineering. Dr. Datta has 25 years of teaching and research experience. His research interest is in the area of materials modelling and optimisation.

Dr. Datta received the Exchange Scientist Award from the Royal Academy of Engineering, UK, and worked at the University of Sheffield, UK. He also worked in the Department of Materials Science and Engineering, Helsinki University of Technology, Finland; the Department of Materials Science and Engineering, Iowa State University, Ames, Iowa, USA; and the Heat Engineering Lab, Department of Chemical Engineering, Åbo Akademi University, Finland, as a visiting scientist. He is currently with SRM University, Kattankulathur, Tamil Nadu, India.

Dr. Datta is a Fellow of the Institution of Engineers (India) and a Life member of the Materials Research Society of India. He is the associate editor of the *Journal of the Institution of Engineers (India): Series D and a member of the editorial board of the International Journal of Materials Engineering Innovation.*

Eight of Dr. Datta's PhD students have been awarded their degrees. He has authored more than 100 publications in journals and peer-reviewed conference proceedings.

1

Introduction

As its title suggests, this book focuses on designing materials through computational methods, with the aid of a group of tools called computational intelligence. We begin by considering the the concept of design in general and then introduce the topic of this book in this chapter.

1.1 Computers and Design

According to the *Merriam-Webster* dictionary (www.merriam-webster.com), the term *design* encompasses activities such as planning and making decisions about something that is being built. A plan can form as a mental process, or take shape on paper (drawings, etc.). Thus design has a broad meaning and can be applied to almost all spheres of life. Whenever we need to develop a product for a focussed purpose, we need to design it first so that it can fulfill the purpose and satisfy the limitations of the available resources for achieving the goal. Thus a proper design process should have two defined aspects: the requirement and the constraints to achieve the requirement.

This clearly indicates that most of the time design leads to development of a product, and whenever we talk about product development it leads to engineering. So it is evident that design is the most important aspect of engineering. Engineering design is the systematic method of applying scientific and mathematical principles to plan the development of a new product having improved required performance or of a manufacturing process that is more efficient than the existing one to produce better quality products, increase productivity, make the production economical or make the process more eco-friendly. The Accreditation Board for Engineering and Technology (ABET), an organisation that accredits education programs in 'applied science, computing, engineering, and engineering technology', defines engineering design as 'the process of devising a system, component, or process to meet desired needs' (ABET 2014, p. 4). It also indicates that designing is basically a decision-making process, in which science and engineering are used to optimally utilise the resources to meet any objective. This is actually a description of an engineering design curriculum, but we can easily use it as an elaborate definition of the concept. The preceding long definition

of engineering design includes validation in addition to objectives and constraints. The engineering product or process designed to achieve particular
objective(s), while considering all of the constraints in the process of achieving them, needs to be validated experimentally. Another important aspect
derives from the definition of engineering design, that is, the use of mathematical sciences during the design process. Mathematical modelling is the
most important tool for any kind of engineering design. Today, with the
development of strong computational facilities, modelling is accompanied
by simulation and optimisation.

Mathematical models can be described as representations of systems
where the relationships between variables are expressed mathematically
(Alder 2001). Variables such as length, weight, temperature, composition
and so forth can be used for developing a model. Modelling can be broadly
divided into two types.

One describes phenomena based on the scientific explanation of the behaviour of the system, and is called an *ab initio*, mechanistic or physical model.
There are two approaches for studying the behaviour of the system from
ab initio models, analytical and numerical. Analytical approaches use calcu-
lus, trigonometry and other mathematical techniques to find the solution.
For complex models, numerical methods are employed, which start with the
initial values of the variables and then find the change over a small inter-
val using equations. On the other hand, in the case of empirical models, the
mathematical relation is developed based on the available experimental or
observed data. The term 'empirical' in science means 'experimental', which
clearly explains the difference from the other type of model. The real advantage of mathematical models is that one can perform virtual 'experiments',
or simulations, using models instead of the real systems. Real experiments
can be expensive and time consuming, and sometimes dangerous, or the
system to be investigated may not even exist yet. In this situation models
can provide the scope to study the system's behaviour under different conditions, virtually. Thus simulations based on a good mathematical model are
important tools for engineering design.

To find the best design that could yield a product or process with the best
performance, we may need to apply optimisation techniques (Deb 1995;
Miettinen 1999) in addition to simulations. The models can act as the objective
functions or the relation that could be used in searching for the best solution.
Constraints against achieving the best design could also be incorporated in
an optimisation process. In real life our demands, targets or objectives are
multiple and conflicting in nature. When we design a car, we try to make it
as comfortable as possible, and simultaneously as economical as possible.
This issue can also be handled using multiobjective optimisation and also
multicriteria decision-making methods. The overall concept of computationally designing a new product is summarised in Figure 1.1. All of these processes can now be easily executed owing to availability of high-performance

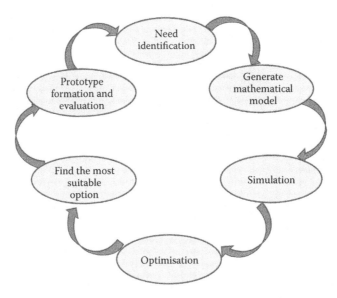

FIGURE 1.1
Engineering design: Computational approach.

computers. Though computers are being extensively used for all types of engineering design, the term computer-aided design (CAD) generally refers to a particular type or a group of software used for designing products for manufacturing. This approach is also used in civil engineering designs, where modelling and simulation are also followed.

The issue of designing high-performance materials computationally, which is the actual subject of this book, is no different from other engineering design issues. Here also we start with the modelling of the materials' properties or other phenomena, and then construct simulations using the models as well as optimisation, single or multiobjective, constrained or unconstrained, to find the best options. There are many approaches to materials modelling. It can be developed from the inherent science of the system, and can be in different length scales (Lee 2011; Lesar 2013). The length scale may vary from the atomistic and molecular level to the domain of crystals, phases, diffusion, recrystallisation, phase transformations and defects to macroscopic assessment of the microstructural features. The tools used are also different for each scale (Figure 1.2). At lower length scales it may be density functional theory and molecular dynamics. Phase-field transformation deals with phases and the phase transformation domain. Finite element analysis can assess the cumulative effect of the microstructure on the final property of the material. These are just a few techniques among the many available.

There is another modelling approach, which deals with the data or observations. The empirical models are quite old in the materials field and have

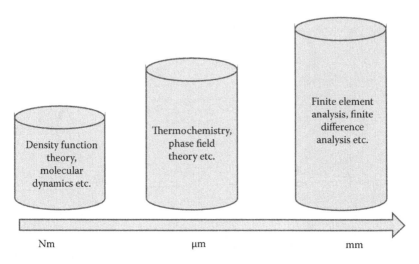

FIGURE 1.2
Different modeling techniques in different length scales.

served significantly in the advancement of materials engineering, particularly in the age-old field of metallurgy. The approach of developing mathematical correlations between the variables using data is quite effective for systems that are complex and the inherent science is not yet fully known. Initially the approach depended solely on statistical methods but computers have made changes possible in this area of materials modelling as well. Several recently invented computational intelligence (CI) techniques have slowly gained importance and become an integrated part of materials modelling and optimisation. Figure 1.3 summarises the approaches of materials modelling. This book concentrates on this particular domain of modelling and optimisation for designing materials.

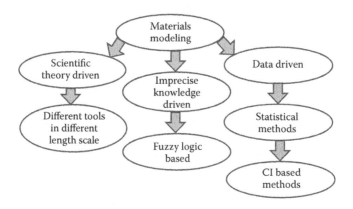

FIGURE 1.3
Different materials modeling approaches.

1.2 Computational Intelligence

Before we define the term *Computational Intelligence*, let us first get a sense of what is meant by intelligence. According to the American Psychological Association (APA), intelligence refers to intellectual functioning. Expanding the definition we can describe intelligence as the ability to learn, understand or to deal with a new and perhaps difficult situation. It is also the ability to apply one's knowledge to influence the surroundings. An intelligent system is one that emulates some aspects of intelligence exhibited in nature, which include learning, adaptability, robustness across problem domains, improving efficiency, information compression and extrapolated reasoning (Rudas and Fodor 2008).

The issue of machine intelligence or artificial intelligence (AI) then arises. In 1950 Alan Turing described the conditions for considering a machine intelligent (Turing 1950). He had a simple logic. If a machine successfully mimics a human to a knowledgeable observer then it may be considered as intelligent. But it seems that the Turing test is one sided. According to him only a machine that passes this test should be considered intelligent. But a machine without sufficient information about humans to imitate a human could still be considered intelligent. According to McCarthy (2007), AI is the science and engineering of making intelligent machines, especially intelligent computer programs. The ultimate goal is to give computer programs a problem-solving capacity similar to that of human beings. Huge improvements in computer science and engineering have led to the invention of systems having intelligent behaviour or features. AI develops an intelligent system by identifying the inherent structure of the problem, and then formal reasoning procedures are applied to describe the structure. Thus AI employs all types of computational techniques to describe the system, as per requirement. But to search and find unknown correlations among the variables for a system not so defined, having inherent complex and nonlinear relationships, a high degree of uncertainty and imprecision need to be accommodated. In such conditions fuzzy logic, artificial neural networks and evolutionary computation are integrated and named computational intelligence (CI). Sometimes additional computational tools are incorporated to make the CI family a bit broader. The IEEE World Congress on Computational Intelligence in 1994 (Orlando, Florida) marked the initiation of such a group of tools. Bezdek (1996) proposed a definition of a system as computationally intelligent if it deals only with numerical (low-level) data, has a pattern recognition component and does not use knowledge as in case of AI. In addition it needs to be computationally adaptive and fault tolerant, having a nearly human-like turnaround and with error rates that approximate human performance. Eberhar and Shi (2007) formulated another definition. According to them CI is defined as a methodology involving computing that exhibits an ability to learn and/or deal with new situations such that the system is perceived to possess one or more attributes of reason, such as generalisation, discovery, association and abstraction. From the preceding definitions it may be stated that CI depends mostly on soft computing techniques, whereas AI also includes hard computing to describe a system. Thus it can be loosely stated that CI is a subset of AI.

The preceding discussion clearly points to the fact that CI is an important tool for dealing with uncertainty and complexity. Most of the practical materials systems have a high degree of complexity and are difficult to describe using conventional tools of materials modelling. CI also has the capacity to discover and extract information, which is very important in terms of design. Almost all of the techniques grouped under CI are covered in this book, with examples of their applications in the field of materials modelling and optimisation towards designing new materials. The most common technique, and also the oldest, is the artificial neural network (ANN; Anderson 1995; Kumar 2004). ANN is a method inspired by biological nervous systems, including the brain, capable of developing highly nonlinear empirical correlations among the independent and response variables. It has a large number of interconnected processing elements, which are highly nonlinear and known as neurons. A biological neuron receives signals from other neurons through the dendrites. The signal is sent through an axon to the synapse, which permits the signal to pass to the other connected neurons. Thus a signal propagates. In the case of ANN, the neurons are replaced by nodes and the efficiency of the synaptic transmission is determined by connection weights. In the case of ANN the weights are adjusted when the relations between the parameters are embedded in the model, a process called learning, as in the case of biological systems (Figure 1.4). ANN is becoming increasingly popular for modelling materials systems, particularly for those in which the final performance of the materials depends on several parameters related in a complicated manner (Datta and Chattopadhyay 2013).

The fuzzy logic (FL) approach to computing is based on 'degrees of truth' rather than the usual Boolean logic of 'true' or 'false' (1 or 0). Thus FL may be expressed as a superset of Boolean logic. It was first introduced by

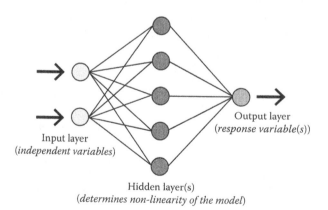

Output layer
(*response variable(s)*)

Input layer
(*independent variables*)

Hidden layer(s)
(*determines non-linearity of the model*)

FIGURE 1.4
Structure of artificial neural network model.

Dr. Lotfi Zadeh in the 1960s as a means to model the uncertainty of natural language (Zadeh 1965). FL is actually a tool to develop the solution of a problem with a tradeoff between significance and precision. A fuzzy inference system employs FL and can exploit imprecise knowledge of a system and be utilised successfully for materials systems. A fuzzy set does not have a crisp or clearly defined boundary. The set contains elements with only a degree of membership; as in FL the truth of any statement becomes a matter of degree. The membership value (or degree of membership) of each point in the input space is mapped to a value between 0 and 1 by a membership function (MF), which is a curve whose shape we can define as a function, and the shape determines the membership value of that variable (Figure 1.5). FL can be used effectively for modelling systems, where impreciseness of the knowledge prevails. The imprecise linguistic rules can be utilised to model the system. On the other hand, easily cognisable imprecise rules can be extracted from the experimental data to make the unknown system transparent to a certain extent, a process known as database mining or knowledge discovery. FL could also be easily hybridised with other CI tools to explore different aspects of the available system information. Though it was a long time before FL attracted the attention of materials engineers, its applications are gaining momentum. There are certain advantages, as discussed previously, that have unlimited potential still waiting to be fully exploited in the materials field. Another approach to deal with uncertainty is the concept of rough sets (RS). RS is a soft computing tool and can be incorporated within CI in a broader sense. The notion of RS was introduced by Zdzisław Pawlak (1982). It is a theory on the logical properties of information systems and has been a methodology of database mining or knowledge discovery in relational databases. In its abstract form, it is another method of dealing with uncertainty mathematically, and is closely related to fuzzy set theory. Rough sets and fuzzy sets can be described as complementary generalisations of classical sets. The approximation spaces of rough set theory are sets with multiple memberships, whereas fuzzy sets describe those with partial memberships. In the rough set concept objects characterised by

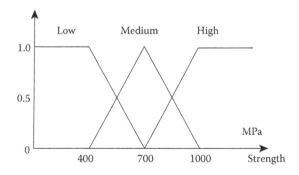

FIGURE 1.5
Fuzzy membership functions.

the same information are indiscernible (similar) in view of the available information. The indiscernibility relation generated in this way is the mathematical basis of rough set theory. Rough set theory can be used for reduction of variables into the minimal set of variables called reducts. The reducts then could be utilised to develop linguistic if–then rules, similar to the FL approach.

Optimisation techniques play an important role in the design of new materials, as discussed earlier. Different evolutionary algorithms such as the genetic algorithm, genetic programming, differential evolution and so forth are acquiring special importance in the design of new materials. All of these techniques have flexible approaches for handling the objective functions and the constraints. The Genetic Algorithm (GA), the oldest and most prominent member of the group of evolutionary algorithms, is a technique which mimics the principles of natural selection, proposed by Charles Darwin, to find the best solution for a problem (Goldberg 2002). GA is actually a stochastic global search method, which operates on a population of feasible solutions initially generated randomly, and tries to evolve the best solution applying the principle of survival of the fittest. At each generation, a new set of solutions is created by the process of selecting fitter individuals and then breeding them. A set of parameter strings, called a chromosome, is treated as an individual solution and a large population of solutions is created with random parameter values. The fitter solutions are bred with each other, where the probability that an individual solution will pass on some of its parameter values to subsequent children is directly related to the fitness of individual (Figure 1.6). As discussed earlier, many real-world optimisation problems

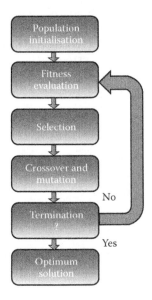

FIGURE 1.6
The genetic algorithm scheme.

have multiple conflicting objectives. In the case of such multiobjective problems, the search is performed following the concept of Pareto-optimality (Deb 2001). In such situations, the concept of an optimum solution is different. A set of solutions providing the best possible compromises between the objectives, known as the Pareto set or front, is treated as the optimum solution, instead of the unique global optimum, as used in the case of the single objective problems.

1.3 Materials Design: Past, Present and Future

The concept of materials design is definitely not new. Civilisation depended enormously on available materials, as evident from the terms historians used to demarcate several periods in the history of civilisation, for example, Stone Age, Bronze Age and Iron Age. Materials engineers designed newer materials, which functioned as important tools for the progress of civilisation. If we look only at a few centuries in the past, when the materials engineering field was taking shape, perhaps in metallurgy or ceramic engineering, we will see that demand for newer materials to accommodate the changing needs of mankind has always been a challenge. Scientists and engineers have tried to develop new materials mostly based on experimental trials. This approach is still prevalent in most of the efforts of developing new materials or improving the properties of existing materials by modifying their composition and/or microstructure. Such a trial-and-error method of searching for new solutions is generally based on some hypothesis. A hypothesis is created based on speculations regarding the outcome of an experiment. The hypothesis is formed through a process called inductive reasoning, which has its basis in the observations leading to a theory. The observation becomes enriched with further experimentation, successful or failed. This improves the understanding of the system and the hypothesis becomes more and more concrete. But the process is tedious, time consuming and expensive. In today's fast changing world the requirements also change quickly. The priority of the materials engineers is to provide civilisation with the materials needed.

With the huge improvement in the experimentation and characterisation facilities in the materials field, now extensive amounts of data are getting generated all over the world. But data have no significance beyond their existence until given a relational connection. This relational database creates information from the data. Today this is also easily achieved using high-end computers and sophisticated tools. The issue of extracting knowledge then arises. Recognising the inherent pattern of the relations in the data is the actual task. The approach of data mining or knowledge discovery using statistical or CI techniques can play a major role in the task. The extracted knowledge could then be utilised to design materials with the required

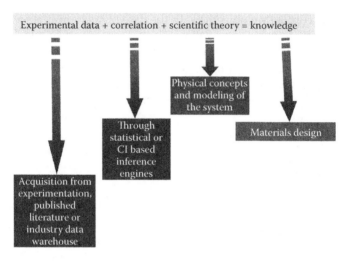

FIGURE 1.7
The scheme of informatics-based design of materials.

properties or performance levels. This approach of engineering design is called 'informatics-based design' in general and termed as 'materials informatics' in particular (Figure 1.7) (Rajan 2005). It could easily reduce the possibility of failure and the time and money spent. Improvements in computational facility have led to the possibility of designing materials using other approaches of mathematical models developed from the inherent physics or chemistry of the system. Such efforts to develop newer materials barring only academic interest will definitely increase with time. Methods of materials design using such models have immense importance in the future direction of the materials discovery. But the discussion in this book is limited to the approach of CI-based materials design.

Barring a few stray efforts the approach of informatics-based design and mechanistic or physical model–based designs have been moving in parallel. The materials community that relies on the fundamental science for modelling feels the absence of science in the informatics-based approach. The section trying to champion the materials informatics domain could not find much practical implications in the other approach. Both sides have their logic and are true in their own way. But the differences will not lead anywhere. These two approaches need to be synergistic rather than competitive. First, the informatics practitioners need to decide that their approach should be limited to those systems in which *ab initio* or other physics-based approaches are not practical. The other group also should seriously take note of the findings of the materials informatics field. The approach of knowledge discovery may lead to findings which may help to remove the limitation of physics-based models to some extent. Developing hybrid systems of scientific and informatics-based modelling is the future for effective materials design. In areas in which knowledge is not precise or only experimental observations are available, CI-based approaches should work hand in hand with the other type of modelling. Such models could be more effective than any of the individual approaches, and shall lead to better materials design.

References

Accreditation Board for Engineering and Technology (ABET). 2014. *Criteria for Accrediting Engineering Programs*. Effective for reviews during the 2015–2016 accreditation cycles.

Alder, M. 2001. *An Introduction to Mathematical Modelling*. HeavenForBooks.com (http://mtm.ufsc.br/~daniel/matap/IntMatMod.pdf).

Anderson, J. A. 1995. *An Introduction to Neural Networks*. Cambridge, MA: MIT Press.

Bender, E. A. 2000. *An Introduction to Mathematical Modeling*. Mineola, NY: Dover Publications.

Bezdek, J. C. 1996. Computational intelligence defined–by everyone! In *Computational Intelligence: Soft Computing and Fuzzy-Neuro Integration with Applications*, ed. O. Kaynak, L. A. Zadeh, B. Türksen and I. J. Rudas, pp. 10–37. Berlin: Springer-Verlag.

Datta, S., and Chattopadhyay, P. P. 2013. Soft computing techniques in advancement of structural metals. *International Materials Reviews* 58: 475–504.

Deb, K. 1995. *Optimization for Engineering Design: Algorithms and Examples*. New Delhi: Prentice-Hall of India.

Deb, K. 2001. *Multi-Objective Optimization using Evolutionary Algorithms*. Hoboken, NJ: John Wiley & Sons.

Eberhar, R. C., and Shi, Y. 2007. *Computational Intelligence Concepts to Implementations*. Burlington, MA: Morgan Kaufmann.

Goldberg, D. E. 2002. *Genetic Algorithms in Search, Optimization and Machine Learning*. New Delhi: Pearson Education.

Kumar, S. 2004. *Neural Networks: A Classroom Approach*. New Delhi: Tata McGraw-Hill.

Lee, J. G. 2011. *Computational Materials Science: An Introduction*. Boca Raton, FL: CRC Press.

Lesar, R. 2013. *Introduction to Computational Materials Science Fundamentals to Applications*. Cambridge, UK: Cambridge University Press.

McCarthy, J. 2007. *Basic Questions, What is Artificial Intelligence?* http://www-formal.stanford.edu/jmc/whatisai/ (Accessed 25 February 2016).

Miettinen, K. 1999. *Nonlinear Multiobjective Optimization*. Boston: Kluwer Academic.

Pawlak, Z. 1982. Rough sets. *International Journal of Computer and Information Sciences* 11: 341–56.

Rajan, K. 2005. Materials Informatics. *Materials Today* 8: 38–45.

Rudas, I. J., and Fodor, J. 2008. Intelligent systems. *International Journal of Computers, Communications & Control* 3: 132–38.

Turing, A. M. 1950. Computing machinery and intelligence. *Mind* 59: 433–60.

Zadeh, L. A. 1965. Fuzzy sets. *Information and Control* 8: 338–53.

2

Conventional Approaches to Materials Design

The concept of computational materials design has grown quickly over the last few decades as a result of the advent of high-power computational facilities. It has become possible for the analytical and numerical methods applied to comparatively large systems to have some real physical significance only because of ever increasing computing facility. Though the field of modelling and simulation for the purpose of materials design is vast, it can be handled on different length and time scales (Janssens et al. 2007). The dominant part of materials modelling is the area where the fundamental physics and chemistry of the system are utilised for modelling the system in different length scales. The modelling approaches are electronic structure and properties of materials determined by *ab initio* and/or semiempirical methods, atomic level properties of materials, thermodynamics-based modelling of phase transformation, microstructure simulations, microstructural level continuum-level modelling and many others. This approach, as expected, combines various tools from both fundamental science and materials engineering and tries to develop a bridge between different length scales. Depending on the length scale there are a number of tools or theories to formulate the models, such as density functional theory; molecular dynamics; thermodynamic modelling, particularly the semiempirical technique for calculation of phase diagrams; phase-field theory; and cellular automata or Monte Carlo techniques for simulation of microstructure and finite element or other continuum methods. There are several other methods also, but only the most frequently used tools are named here and discussed briefly in this chapter. In addition to the science-based mathematical models there are also data-driven models. The statistical models are discussed in Chapter 3, and computational intelligence (CI)-based tools of data-driven modelling are covered in Chapters 4 and 5. As the focus of this book is on the CI-based techniques, a very brief account of the conventional and most prevalent materials modelling and simulation techniques is given here.

2.1 Density Functional Theory

Density functional theory (DFT), a computational quantum mechanical modelling method, forms the basis of a diversified and active area of present-day materials research in atomic, molecular, solid state and even nuclear physics (Eschrig 2003; Jones 2015). DFT determines the properties of a multi-electron system by using functionals (functions of another function) or the spatially dependent electron density, through investigation of the ground state electronic structure of multi-body systems. From its introduction in the mid-1960s, DFT has become one of the most popular methods used in materials engineering since the 1990s, chiefly for two reasons. First, the theory was greatly refined to capture better the exchange and correlation interactions, which were initially absent in the concept. Second, a high-end computational facility was the prerequisite for an effective utilisation of the theory, which previously was not easily available. The modifications include a capacity to deal with spin polarised systems, multicomponent systems such as nuclei and electron hole droplets, free energy at finite temperatures, superconductors with electronic pairing mechanisms, relativistic electrons, time-dependent phenomena and excited states, bosons, molecular dynamics and so forth. The conceptual root of DFT lies in the Thomas–Fermi model, which was proposed in 1927. It provides a functional form for the kinetic energy of a noninteracting electron gas in some known external potential, possibly due to impurities, as a function of the density. It is a local density functional and becomes exact for a uniform electron gas. The early concept of a density functional was put on a theoretical footing by the Hohenberg–Kohn theorems, which state that for any system of interacting particles in an external potential, the density is uniquely determined. Thus the external potential is a unique functional of the density. They further describe how a universal functional for the energy can be defined in terms of the density, where the exact ground state is the global minimum value of this functional. These theorems can be applied to the time domain to develop a 'time-dependent density functional theory', which is generally used to describe excited states. The Kohn–Sham theory reduces the intractable multibody problem of interacting electrons in a static external to a tractable problem of noninteracting electrons moving in an effective potential. The Hohenberg–Kohn theorems are used in this context to minimise the total energy with respect to the orbitals to obtain the orbitals that give rise to the ground state energy (Fiolhais et al. 2003).

DFT can calculate structural properties such as lattice parameters, elastic constants, atomic forces, equilibrium geometry, defect structures and lattice dynamics related issues such as vibrational frequencies, vibrational entropy, electronic structure, band structure, density of states, and so forth. These abilities of DFT make it suitable for the interpretation and prediction of complex system behaviour at an atomic scale. Recently DFT has been applied to find the effects of dopants on phase transformation of oxides and magnetic behaviour in dilute magnetic semiconductors.

2.2 Molecular Dynamics

In the length scale of materials modelling the concept of molecular dynamics (MD) comes after the concept of DFT, though there are numerous examples of combined applications of both the techniques. But generally speaking MD is a technique for simulation of complex systems at the atomic or molecular level (Haile 1997). The concept of MD was initially based on solving the classical equations of motion numerically to study the time evolution of the system. The time evolution of a system of interacting particles (atoms, molecules, granules, etc.) can be computed using this technique. The atoms and molecules interact for a period of time, providing some idea about the motion of the particles. Initially a set condition including the initial positions and velocities of the particles and interaction potential for deriving the forces among the particles is set. Then the evolution of dynamics of the system with time is followed by solving a set of equations for all the particles. Though this is the original variance of MD, other types were introduced in the 1980s: 'quantum' or 'first-principles' MD simulations, which take the quantum nature of the chemical bond into account (Baker and Norris 2015). Long simulations even for classic MD are mathematically difficult, as the cumulative errors in numerical integration generate problems. In the case of quantum MD the density function for the valence electrons that determine bonding is computed using quantum equations, whereas the dynamics of ions are analysed using classical mechanics. The advent of this quantum MD simulation brought an important improvement over the classical approach and started finding applications in biological problems also. It is evident that quantum MD requires more computational resources in comparison to the classical MD (Frenkel 2002).

MD is now used to model three-dimensional structures of proteins and other macromolecules. In Figure 2.1 MD is used to simulate an antiferroelectric liquid crystalline molecule, MHOBC. MD can also be used to simulate the dynamics of atomic-level phenomena such as thin film growth and ion subplantation. In biophysics and system biology, the method is applied for ligand docking and simulations of lipid layers.

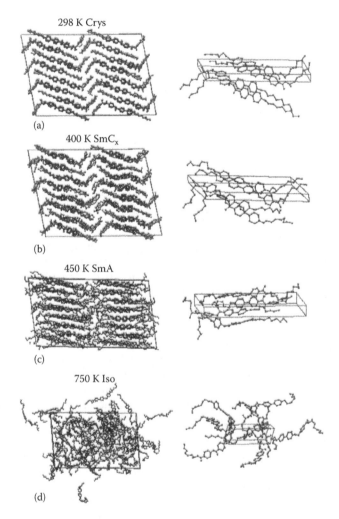

298 K Crys

(a)

400 K SmC$_x$

(b)

450 K SmA

(c)

750 K Iso

(d)

FIGURE 2.1

The molecular packing structure of antiferroelectric liquid crystalline molecule, MHPOBC calculated by MD simulation at (a) 298 K, (b) 400 K, (c) 450 K and (d) 750 K. (From Toriumi, H. et al. *Molecular Crystals and Liquid Crystals* 402: 31–42, 2003. With permission.)

2.3 Thermodynamic Modelling and the CALPHAD Approach

Concepts of thermodynamics and its solutions are of immense importance for computational modelling of phase transformation and microstructure evolution (Perrut 2015). Thermodynamic approaches are a powerful methodology for describing microscopic changes in the materials, for example, solidification, recrystallisation, grain growth, phase transformation in different conditions, and so forth. In this field also the arrival of high-powered computers has made successful ventures into the study of thermodynamic properties, from binary and ternary alloys to more complicated but relevant systems. This has led to the evolution of a field called computational thermodynamics (CT), which has slowly become indispensable in the field of materials design. Even CT is being extensively used in industry for designing alloy composition and heat treatment parameters. In an extension of CT, along with comprehensive thermodynamic databases, the CALculation of PHAse Diagrams (CALPHAD) technique was developed.

Gibbs free energy G of a system calculated as a function of temperature, pressure and chemical composition gives a complete description of the thermodynamic behaviour of the system. If G can be calculated the thermodynamic equilibrium can also be calculated by minimising G. Then for any system the stable phases at a particular temperature, pressure and composition can be calculated, and that will lead to development of any phase diagram. This is the main idea behind CALPHAD, where the free energy of every phase is calculated by certain polynomials, called Redlich–Kistler polynomials (Tedenac et al. 2004). The adjustable parameters of the polynomial are evaluated by comparing the prediction of the polynomial with the collected experimental and theoretical information available on phase equilibria. The optimised parameters are utilised for the final prediction and construction of the phase diagram, as well as the thermodynamic properties of the phases, as shown in Figure 2.2. In the case of ternary and higher-order systems, the ternary Gibbs excess energy is generally added. The reliability of the prediction depends on the available experimental database. A set of data developed through *ab initio* calculations using DFT is also being used.

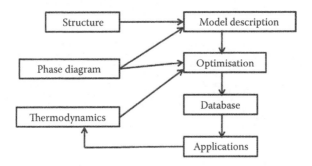

FIGURE 2.2
The CALPHAD method.

2.4 Phase-Field Simulation

Phase-field models are mathematical models for solving interfacial problems and have become popular to describe a host of free-boundary problems in various areas of materials research (Provatas and Elder 2010). The areas include development of microstructures during solidification and solid-state transformations. In all cases there is motion of interfaces or boundaries between the phases. Here diffuse-interface theories replace the classical sharp interface with continuous variations of order parameters, such as density, and somehow maintaining similarity with microscopic theories of interfaces. Thus in phase-field models the diffuseness of the interface is the key point and the interfaces are described by continuous scalar fields having constant values in the bulk phases, which vary continuously but steeply across the diffuse front or interface.

Phase-field models are generally classified into two groups based on the treatment of the diffuse interfaces. In the Cahn and Hilliard approach (Anderson et al. 2000), the interface is treated as a coarse-graining of the inherent atomistic configuration. The width of the interface is made identical to its physical width, which is quite small. This makes it a thermodynamically consistent simulation approach, with the size matching the actual microstructures. But this simulation requires a good computational facility, as there is a huge difference in the dimensions of the matrix and the interface. As the algorithm is made capable of calculating small interfaces, it needs huge computation for the large matrix. In the second approach, the phase field solves the underlying free boundary problem. Here the computational width exceeds the actual to make the numerical computation easy. An example of phase-field simulation of solidification is shown in Figure 2.3.

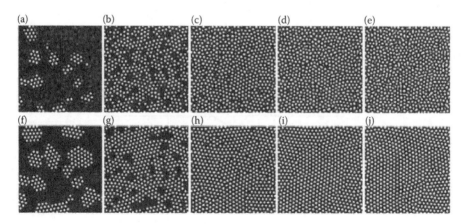

FIGURE 2.3
Solidification in phase field simulations, where (a–e) early stages of solidification and (f–j) later stage of solidification. (From Gránásy, L. et al. *Philosophical Magazine* 91: 123–149, 2011. With permission.)

2.5 Cellular Automata and Monte Carlo Simulations

Cellular automata (CA) describe the spatial and temporal evolution of a complex system by applying some transformation rules through a predefined lattice system (Codd 1968), which is nothing but an array of nodes (cells) of some dimension. This lattice may be of any dimension, and is of infinite extent. In the case of two-dimensional CA all the points are in a plane and have only integral coordinates. Even for higher dimensional CA, each point in *n*-dimensional Euclidean space has all integral coordinates. The transformation rules determine the state of a site or node, as a function of its previous state and the state of the neighbouring sites. The rules can be local or global, deterministic or probabilistic or even fuzzy in nature. CA models are applied to fluid dynamics, plasma physics, chemical systems, solidification, and many other fields. The changes in the microstructure in the case of high-temperature deformation of steel due to dynamic recrystallisation are shown in Figure 2.4.

The Monte Carlo (MC) method reaches the solution of a problem as a parameter of a hypothetical population, which is constructed using random numbers (James 1980). Thus the MC method can be applied where there is similarity between the desired result and the expected behaviour of a stochastic system. As in CA, here also a rule, based on some reasonable mathematical and/or physical theory, needs to be available to decide the outcome of such a stochastic trial. For the materials community it is a method used to study the statistical physics of a phase equilibrium. The MC method has been successfully applied to simulate microstructural evolution describing the equilibrium on a local basis, to study the kinetics of the processes that lead to equilibrium

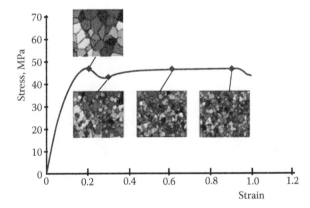

FIGURE 2.4

CA simulation of microstructural evolution for HY-100 steel deformed at 1100°C. (Reprinted from *Materials Science and Engineering*, A365, Qian, M., and Guo, Z. X. Cellular automata simulation of microstructural evolution during dynamic recrystallization of an HY-100 steel, pp. 180–85, Copyright 2004, with permission from Elsevier.)

as a function of time, as in cases of grain growth or recrystallisation (Chun et al. 2006). A microstructure can be mapped onto a two-dimensional (2D) or three-dimensional (3D) lattice. Grain growth at a heat-affected zone of a welded structure of steel is simulated using MC as shown in Figure 2.5.

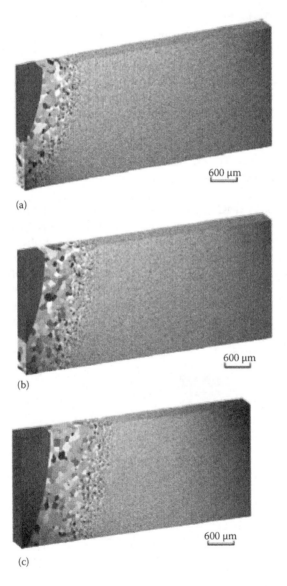

600 µm

(a)

600 µm

(b)

600 µm

(c)

FIGURE 2.5
MC simulation of heat affected zone microstructure of ultrafine grain steel with (a) low, (b) medium and (c) high heat inputs. (Reprinted from *Computational Materials Science*, 31, Shi, Y., Chen, D., Lei, Y., and Li, X. HAZ microstructure simulation in welding of aultrafine grain steel, pp. 379–88, Copyright 2004, with permission from Elsevier.)

2.6 Finite Element and Other Similar Methods

Numerical solutions of mathematical problems described by partial differential equations (PDEs) could be achieved by the three classical choices: the finite difference method (FDM), the finite volume method (FVM) and the finite element method (FEM) (Yip 2005). FDM is based on the Taylor expansion for approximating the differential equations. It uses a topologically square network of lines to develop the discretisation of the PDE. This kind of network is not suitable for complex geometries in multiple dimensions. To solve this problem the other two methods of discretisation evolved. FVM uses a volume integral formulation of the problem with a finite partitioning set of volumes to discretise the PDE. It is used mostly in computational fluid dynamics problems.

The FEM is the most popular discretisation technique in structural mechanics. The basic concept of FEM is the subdivision of the mathematical model into disjoint components of simple geometry called finite elements (Suli 2000; Liu and Quek 2013). The response of each element is expressed in terms of a finite number of degrees of freedom, described as the value of unknown function(s) at the nodal points. In this way the response of the mathematical model is approximated by connecting or assembling the responses of all elements. The finite elements do not overlap in space. In FEM the properties of the elements go by the name disjoint support or local support, and finite elements of different types can be used. The local properties of the elements can also be calculated by considering them in isolation. The steps for FE analysis of the microstructure of the intermetallic layers formed during soldering of Cu are shown in Figure 2.6.

2.7 Multiscale Modelling and Integrated Computational Materials Engineering

The tools described in the preceding text are only the major tools used in different length scales of materials modelling. There are many more. These tools could be used effectively in tandem to develop a complete modelling of composition–processing–structure–property correlation for a material, where the outcome of the lower length scale models can be used as inputs for the higher length scale. In this way of using the techniques in series, the analytical and numerical concepts could be used for materials design. The idea of multiscale modelling was coined a few decades ago, where the outputs of a lower scale of models are utilised as the inputs of a higher scale of models. In that way it will be possible to develop mathematical relations for the

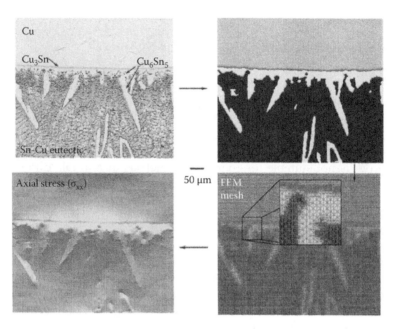

FIGURE 2.6
The steps of FE analysis starting from the original microstructure, segmentation of the image, meshing and finally the stress state. (Reprinted from *Materials Characterization*, 49, Chawla, N., Patel, B. V., Koopman, M., Chawla, K. K., Saha, R., Patterson, B. R., Fuller, E. R., and Langer, S. A. Microstructure-based simulation of thermomechanical behavior of composite materials by object-oriented finite element analysis, pp. 395–407, Copyright 2003, with permission from Elsevier.)

behaviours of materials at the atomic scale to the final microstructure. This will enable design of materials with the required properties from the atomic level. But such efforts are still limited to some simple systems. There are certain limitations in these concepts; they mostly depend on simplifications and assumptions about the materials system to varied extents. These can make the outcome of the models far removed from the real situation without any practical implications. In such cases other concepts such as informatics and imprecise knowledge of the system should be incorporated with the help of statistics or CI techniques. In recent years the concept of integrated computational materials engineering (ICME) (Horstemeyer 2012) has been introduced, in which the limitation of the previous approach was overcome through an integrated approach where both physical as well as empirical and semiempirical methods of modelling were used to develop practical platforms for designing materials with improved performance. ICME is targeted to provide a holistic system for accelerated materials development, design optimisation and manufacturing. It approaches the materials design, development and manufacturing of products together.

References

Anderson, D. M., McFadden, G. B., and Wheeler, A. A. 2000. A phase-field model of solidification with convection. *Physica D* 135:175–94.

Baker, C. H., and Norris, P. M. 2015. Effect of long- and short-range order on SiGe alloy thermal conductivity: Molecular dynamics simulation. *Physical Review B* 91: 180302(R).

Chawla, N., Patel, B. V., Koopman, M., Chawla, K. K., Saha, R., Patterson, B. R., Fuller, E. R., and Langer, S. A. 2003. Microstructure-based simulation of thermomechanical behavior of composite materials by object-oriented finite element analysis. *Materials Characterization* 49: 395–407.

Chun, Y. B., Semiatin, S. L., and Hwang, S. K. 2006. Monte Carlo modeling of microstructure evolution during the static recrystallization of cold-rolled, commercial-purity titanium. *Acta Materialia* 54: 3673–89.

Codd, E. F. 1968. *Cellular Automata*. Orlando, FL: Academic Press.

Eschrig, H. 2003. *The Fundamentals of Density Functional Theory*. Leipzig: Edition am Gutenbergplatz Leipzig.

Fiolhais, C., Nogueira, F., and Marques, M. (Eds.). 2003. *A Primer in Density Functional Theory*. Berlin: Springer-Verlag.

Frenkel, D. 2002. *Understanding Molecular Simulations – From understanding to applications*, 2nd ed. San Diego, CA: Academic Press.

Gránásy, L., Tegze, G., Tóth, G. I., and Pusztai, T. 2011. Phase field crystal modelling of crystal nucleation, heteroepitaxy and patterning. *Philosophical Magazine* 91:123–149.

Haile, J. M. 1997. *Molecular Dynamics Simulation: Elementary Methods*. New York: Wiley-Interscience.

Horstemeyer, M. F. 2012. *Integrated Computational Materials Engineering (ICME) for Metals: Using Multiscale Modeling to Invigorate Engineering Design with Science*. Hoboken, NJ: John Wiley & Sons.

James, F. 1980. Monte Carlo theory and practice. *Reports on Progress in Physics* 43: 1145–89.

Janssens, K. G. F., Raabe, D., Kozeschnik, E., Miodownik, M. A., and Nestler, B. 2007. *Computational Materials Engineering: An Introduction to Microstructure Evolution*. Amsterdam: Elsevier.

Jones, R. O. 2015. Density functional theory: Its origins, rise to prominence, and future. *Reviews of Modern Physics* 87: 897–924.

Liu, G. R., and Quek, S. S. 2013. *The Finite Element Method: A Practical Course*. Oxford: Butterworth-Heinemann.

Perrut, M. 2015. Thermodynamic modeling by the CALPHAD method and its applications to innovative materials. *Aerospace Lab Journal* 9: 1–11.

Provatas, N., and Elder, K. 2010. *Phase-Field Methods in Materials Science and Engineering*. Weinheim, Germany: Wiley-VCH.

Qian, M., and Guo, Z. X. 2004. Cellular automata simulation of microstructural evolution during dynamic recrystallization of an HY-100 steel. *Materials Science and Engineering* A365: 180–85.

Shi, Y., Chen, D., Lei, Y., and Li, X. 2004. HAZ microstructure simulation in welding of a ultrafine grain steel. *Computational Materials Science* 31: 379–88.

Suli, E. 2000. Lecture Notes on Finite Element Methods for Partial Differential Equations. Mathematical Institute, University of Oxford.

Tedenac, J. C., Li, H., Gomes-Fries, S., Record, M. C., Marin-Ayral, R. M., and Ravot, D. 2004. Phase diagram calculation, a tool for design of thermoelectric materials. A Calphad contribution to multicomponent antimonide-based systems. In *Proceedings of the 2nd European Conference on Thermoelectrics of European Thermoelectric Society*, KrakÃƒÂ³w, Poland, pp. 216–21. http://home.agh.edu.pl/~ets2004/proceedings/Tedenac.pdf (Accessed 19 March 2016).

Toriumi, H., Yoshida, M., Kamiya, N., and Takeuchi, M. 2003. Molecular Dynamics Simulation of an Antiferroelectric Liquid Crystalline Molecule MHPOBC: Conformational Transition in Smectic Phases. *Molecular Crystals and Liquid Crystals* 402: 31–42.

Yip, S. (Ed.). 2005. *Handbook of Materials Modeling*, Vol. I: *Methods and Models* (pp. 1–32). Dordrecht, the Netherlands: Springer-Verlag.

3

Statistics and Data Mining Concepts in Materials Design

We very briefly discussed the scientific theory-driven modelling of materials systems in Chapter 2. In this chapter we begin to discuss the use of experimental or industrial data in materials modelling. Though the discussion is limited to statistical methods, still not in the domain of computational intelligence (CI), insight into this type of modelling is absolutely necessary to finally understand the CI tools and their applications. In the field of materials modelling, especially in the case of modelling complex metallic systems, statistical modelling concepts, particularly regression analysis, have been used in developing predictive models for materials properties, transformation temperatures and also process variables for the past eight decades, if not longer. After the introduction of artificial neural networks in the field of materials modelling, statistical regression analysis took a back seat in the development of new models. However, the existing models have huge practical relevance even in today's world of metallurgy. But in this era of high-capacity computers, the statistical concepts in materials engineering have become more relevant than before in the form of data mining, taking the form and shape of 'materials informatics'. This chapter therefore begins with a brief description of statistical linear regression techniques and the past applications of the techniques in the metallurgical field. The concept of data mining is then introduced, followed by a few accounts of its recent applications in the materials field.

3.1 An Overview of Statistical Modelling in the Materials Field

In most metallurgical processes regression analyses are used, where data are best fitted to a specified relationship, which is usually linear (Vittal and Malini 2012). Several types of linear regression analyses are available:

- Simple linear regression: one dependent variable, one independent variable
- Multiple linear regression: one dependent variable, two or more independent variables

- Logistic regression: one dependent variable (binary), two or more independent variables
- Ordinal regression: one dependent variable (ordinal), one or more independent variable(s)
- Multinominal regression: one dependent variable (nominal), one or more independent variable(s)
- Discriminant analysis: one dependent variable (nominal), one or more independent variable(s)

Among all of these methods multiple linear regression analysis is the method which drew huge applications in the materials field as noted previously. Multiple linear regression attempts to model the relationship between two or more independent variables and a dependent or response variable by fitting a linear equation to the data (Chatterjee and Hadi 2013). Every value of the independent variable x is associated with a value of the dependent variable y. The population regression line, which summarises the trend in the population between the independent variable x and the mean of the responses, for p number of input or independent variables $x_1, x_2,..., x_p$ is defined to be $\mu_y = \beta_0 + \beta_1 x_1 + \beta_2 x_2 + ... + \beta_p x_p$. The observed values for y vary about their means μ_y and are assumed to have the standard deviation σ. The multiple regression model includes a term to incorporate this residual variation, ε. Thus the model for multiple linear regression for n observations in the data is $y_i = \beta_0 + \beta_1 x_{i1} + \beta_2 x_{i2} + ... + \beta_p x_{ip} + \varepsilon_i$ for $i = 1, 2, ... n$. The error is calculated in the form of means square error to estimate $b_0, b_1, ... b_p$, the final set of coefficients for the p inputs. Sometimes higher order polynomial terms, particularly the quadratic terms, are added to this type of equation to capture a nonlinear system.

This concept is applied in different fields of metallurgical systems, but most widely in that of ferrous alloys, particularly steel. Let us first consider the case of predictive models for phase transformation temperature, an important aspect for designing steel. The start and finish of equilibrium austenitisation temperatures were first proposed by Grange in 1961, and it was in the form of

$$Ae_1 = 1333 - 25 \text{ Mn} + 40 \text{ Si} + 42 \text{ Cr} - 26 \text{ Ni}$$

$$Ae_3 = 1570 - 323 \text{ C} - 25 \text{ Mn} + 80 \text{ Si} - 3 \text{ Cr} - 32 \text{ Ni},$$

where the temperature is described in °F and the elements in wt%. With time the equation was modified again and again by other researchers through addition of new terms describing the effect of other alloying elements and also modification of the coefficients of the existing elements. Ac_1 and Ac_3, the start and finish austenitisation temperatures during heating, are also modelled in the same way. The equation changed with time and even quadratic terms were added. Predictive models for the start and finish austenitisation temperature during cooling (Ar_1 and Ar_3), bainite transformation start and finish temperature (B_s and B_f) and martensite transformation start and finish temperature (M_s and M_f) were also developed. The carbon equivalent is an important measure of steel for welding purposes and the regression model for that also changed with time with the addition of new elements. The hardness of steel at different heat treatment conditions, the strength of the steel taking into account the composition and a few microstructural features have been predicted by many researchers. These equations are adequately collected in the *Steel Forming and Heat Treating Handbook* by Gorni (2009). On one hand, the equations developed in this method are more or less transparent in nature and automatically provide some idea about the role of the variables through the coefficients, though in a very crude way. But the difficulties associated with this type of linear regression analysis are

- A relationship has to be chosen before analysis.
- The relationship chosen tends to be linear, or with nonlinear terms added together.
- Once derived, the same relation applies across the entire span of the input space. This is not applicable for all cases. For example, the relationship between strength and the carbon concentration of an iron base alloy changes radically as steel goes to cast iron (Bhadeshia 1999).

3.2 Concept of Data Mining

In the age of information huge amounts of data are generated in all fields of life. This growth of available data is mainly due to the fast development of powerful data collection and storage tools, particularly computers. Data mining turns a large collection of data into knowledge. It searches for knowledge (interesting patterns) in data (Liu and Motoda 2007), and therefore the term 'data mining' does not reflect the actual sense of the concept. The meaning of coal mining is obtaining coal from the ground. But in data mining the data are not mined; on the contrary it is actually knowledge mining from data, knowledge extraction and data or pattern analysis. Another popular term for this is knowledge discovery from data (KDD). The process of data mining needs the following steps for successful extraction of knowledge (Figure 3.1):

1. Data cleaning, meant for removing noise and inconsistent data
2. Data integration, for combining data from multiple sources
3. Data selection, to select the relevant data from the available sources

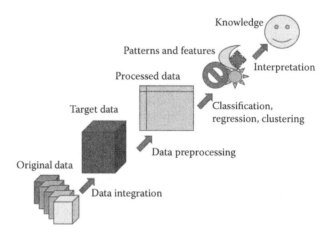

FIGURE 3.1
Steps of extracting knowledge from data.

4. Data transformation, transforming data appropriate in a form suit-able for application of the mining tools
5. Data mining, when the tools and techniques for mining are employed
6. Pattern evaluation, for identifying the important patterns evolved from the data
7. Knowledge presentation, needed for presenting the extracted knowl-edge in the proper form

The data sources for data mining in the field of materials engineering may be the published experimental data, data generated by sophisticated charac-terisation tools and stored in computers, data warehouses of industries and the web and other information repositories. The methods for knowledge dis-covery come from statistics as well as computational intelligence methods. Different tools are used for different purposes. Let us briefly look at all of these tools and the purpose of using them.

- *Classification*: In this process a model (or function) is developed which describes the classes or concepts of data. The model is used to pre-dict the class label of objects for which the class label is not known. It can be presented using classification rules (in the form of if–then rules), decision trees, mathematical formulae, support vector machines, *k*-nearest-neighbour classification or neural networks. A decision tree, a well-established statistical technique, is a flowchart-like tree struc-ture, where each node denotes the role of any attribute on the output classes, with the tree leaves representing classes or class distributions.
- *Regression*: The classification techniques have the capability for pre-dicting categorical labels; regression models deal with continuous

outputs. The concept of regression has already been discussed in this chapter.

- *Cluster analysis*: Unlike classification and regression, clustering analyses data without any target class or output values. In this case the objects are clustered or grouped based on intraclass similarity and interclass dissimilarity. Thus compared to classification and regression techniques, clustering can be considered an unsupervised learning technique.

3.3 Mining Materials Data and Informatics-Based Design

The ultimate target of all these tools for knowledge extraction could be broadly divided into two parts. The first is finding the variables in the input space that have an important or significant role in controlling the output, called the feature selection, and second is finding the roles they play individually or in combination with other variables and developing a mathematically expressed correlation. These two aspects can be dealt with using existing statistical techniques or by computational techniques. In the field of materials design also there are several examples of such research where materials data have been used for data mining purposes, leading to informatics-based design of materials, using both types of tools (Rajan 2005). As this book focusses on the CI-based aspects of computational materials design, applications of those tools are discussed in all chapters. In this chapter, the application of regression analysis in the materials field has already been discussed, and now some more applications will be discussed in the domain of classification and clustering and for the sake of feature selection.

3.3.1 Hot Rolled Steel Plate Classification

This is a typical application of data mining in industrial data, where the purpose is to find the root cause of diversion of hot rolled steel plates at the end of the rolling process that results in an off-grade product failing to achieve the required properties (Das et al. 2006). Finding the cause is a kind of feature selection, which will lead to selection of the proper composition of steel to avoid rejection and improve the productivity of the plates. The techniques used here are linear discriminant analysis (LDA), Classification and Regression Tree (CART) – a method for developing decision tree, k-means clustering and Partition Around Medoid (PAM) clustering. The data has the chemistry, namely carbon, manganese, sulphur, phosphorus and silicon as inputs and the status of steel plates (accepted or rejected) as the output. The other variables, including the hot rolling process variables, which remain constant for all cases, are not considered.

Discriminant analysis develops weighted summations, usually a linear combination and called a linear discriminant function, of the discriminating variables or features in such a way that it best describes the differences between the groups or classes (Rencher 2002). The values of this combination for cases within a group are fairly similar and between groups are most dissimilar. After performing the aforementioned analysis on the given rolled steel data set, we get the Linear Discrimination Function (LDF) as

$$LDF = -798.399 + 1365.19 \text{ (Si)} + 14{,}264.204 \text{ (P)} + 540.422 \text{ (Mn)} + 1580.087 \text{ (C)}$$

The prior probabilities for the two groups are 0.594 and 0.406. The group centroids for 'OK' and 'Diverted' groups are found to be 1.213 and −1.777 respectively. From the LDF it is evident that discriminant analysis has shown a positive effect of carbon, manganese, silicon, and phosphorus on the strength of the steel, whereas it has neglected the effect of sulphur on it. This finding is also acceptable from a metallurgical point of view. Sulphur has a detrimental effect predominantly because of the formation of sulphide inclusions.

A decision tree divides the input spaces of a data set into mutually exclusive regions. Each variable is assigned a value which separates the data into branches of a tree. The tree has internal and external nodes connected by branches. An internal node is a decision-making unit that decides which child node will appear next. The external nodes, also known as the leaves or terminal nodes, have no child nodes. This procedure consists of two parts – first the tree growing, and then tree pruning and shrinking (Brieman et al. 1984). CART grows a decision tree by determining a succession of splits that partitions the training data into disjoint sets. The tree usually becomes too large based on the training data set, resulting in a high degree of accuracy in predicting the training data but losing generalisation capability, called overfitting. In such situations, the weakest subtree, measured by the training error and the number of terminal nodes, is pruned. Shrinking reduces the number of nodes by fitting the values of child nodes with their parent nodes.

The results of CART analysis are shown in Figure 3.2 in the form of a decision tree. The number of terminal nodes is 6. The misclassification error rate is found to be 7.25%. According to the tree to distinguish an 'OK' heat from a 'Diverted' one Mn is the most important factor. The importance of Si, P and C follow in order of importance. Here again it is seen that the role of S is found to be insignificant.

The next technique employed for the classification is cluster analysis (Johnson and Wichern 1982; Everitt et al. 2001). The clustering algorithms fall into two categories. A partitioning algorithm is a method that divides the data set into k clusters, where the integer k needs to be specified by the user, whereas

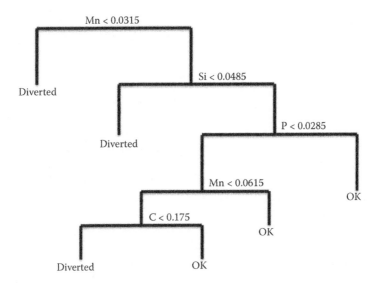

FIGURE 3.2
Optimal decision tree from CART analysis.

a hierarchical algorithm describes a method yielding an entire hierarchy of clustering for the given data set. In the present work the partitioning algorithm for clustering is used. The most commonly used partitioning methods are k-means clustering and PAM clustering. In k-means clustering the observations are classified into one of k groups. The groups are determined by calculating the centroid (using least squares) for each group and assigning each observation to the group with the centroid closest to it. The PAM algorithm is similar to k-means but uses medoids rather than centroids. PAM will first compute a dissimilarity matrix from the data. The algorithm computes k representative objects, called medoids, which together determine a cluster. The number k of clusters is an argument of the function. Cluster analysis by k-means and two types of PAM used in this work revealed that for C, Mn and Si the values are high for the rolled product being 'OK', and for S the values are low. The only visible difference in all these cluster analyses from that of the previous ones is that they could not confirm the significance of P.

Now let us discuss the case of using the Mahalanobis–Taguchi system (MTS) for the same steel data (Das and Datta 2007). In the MTS approach, the Mahalanobis distance (MD) (Mahalanobis 1936) is used to measure the degree of abnormality of patterns, and principles of Taguchi methods (Taguchi and Jugulum 2002) are used to evaluate the accuracy of the predictions based on the scale constructed. Taguchi proposed the use of Mahalanobis distance in multidimensional systems for prediction, diagnosis and pattern recognition, without any distribution assumption, and attempted a selection of features.

The concept of orthogonal array (OA) and signal-to-noise (S/N) ratio is incorporated to find useful variables and a threshold for future diagnosis. In the MTS, the Mahalanobis space (reference group) is obtained using the standardised variables of healthy or normal data. The Mahalanobis space (MS) can be used to discriminate between normal and abnormal data. Once this MS is established, the number of variables or attributes is reduced using OA and the S/N ratio by evaluating the contribution of each attribute. The different stages of the MTS method are summarised as (1) construction of a measurement scale with Mahalanobis space as a reference and (2) validation of the measurement scale. In Figure 3.3a, a range of C in a 'normal' group is considered. Values of other variables were fixed at their average levels for both the groups. The differences in MD values between the normal and

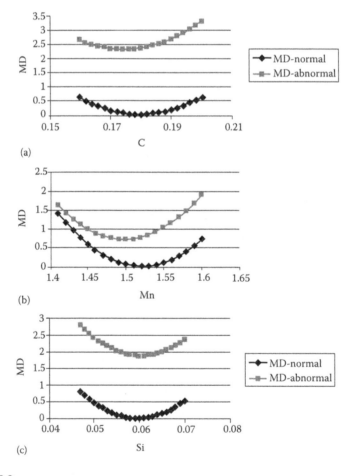

FIGURE 3.3
Change in MD vs. change in (a) C %, (b) Mn %, (c) Si % of the 'normal' group. *(Continued)*

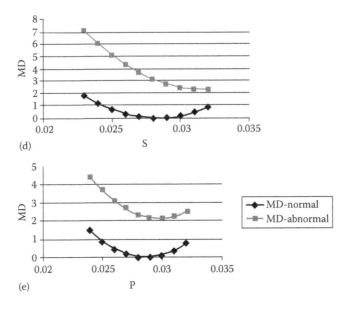

FIGURE 3.3 (CONTINUED)
Change in MD vs. change in (d) S % and (e) P % of the 'normal' group. (Reprinted from *Computational Materials Science*, 38, Das, P., and Datta, S. Exploring the effects of chemical composition in hot rolled steel product using Mahalanobis distance scale under Mahalanobis–Taguchi system, pp. 671–77, Copyright 2007, with permission from Elsevier.)

the abnormal groups are seen to be almost the same for the whole range of C. Figure 3b–e describes the changes in MD values with Mn, Si, S and P. Though the nature of the curves for Si and P are similar to that of C, it is observed that the MD values of the two groups come closer to each other for lower Mn content and higher S content. These findings indicate that because of changes in the C, Si and P content in the steel, the steel does not change its group. But at lower Mn content and higher Si content the behaviour of the steel becomes such that it becomes difficult to distinguish between the OK and Diverted groups. This clearly points to the fact that Mn and S are the two most important variables or features. This also almost corroborates the results of the previous techniques employed on these data, as mentioned earlier. The application of several statistical data mining techniques in parallel can surely bring out the hidden pattern and solve many critical problems, such as the steel design problem of this work.

3.3.2 High-Temperature Superconductors

This is a case of application of Principal Component Analysis (PCA) in materials data for designing high-temperature superconductors (Suh et al. 2002). PCA is a technique to reduce the dimensionality of the data and select the important features of a system. In many systems the variables are inter-related and a Principal Component (PC) can be described as a new variable developed from a linear combination of the correlated variables. The first PC describes a term which has maximum influence on the output. The second PC is orthogonal (uncorrelated) to the first and accounts for most of the remaining variance, and so on. Thus the dimensionality of the data is reduced and prediction or classification is made easier in this new space. In the area of computational materials design the application of PCA is slowly gaining ground. This work focusses on the superconductivity of MgB_2 and tries to find the factors that govern this characteristic of this compound. The average number of valence electrons, electronegativity difference, radii difference, elemental concentration/mole fraction stoichiometry, cohesive energy and ionisation energy are considered as the attributes for all high-temperature superconducting materials. Then the data are subjected to PCA to find the important attributes and in that respect find the reason behind high-temperature superconductivity of MgB_2.

PCA analysis for all sets of compounds, namely the intermetallic systems, shows the presence of a strong eigen component in the data set. It shows that MgB_2 appears to be clustered around the response behavior space near other known superconductors. The exercise finds the potential variables for describing the systems and also provides hints on how new chemistries may influence the structure in the case of superconductivity.

Further PCA analyses of the data for an additional 34 similar AB_2 alloys were performed. A few typical score plots are shown in Figure 3.4, where the data points of the relevant crystal structure are highlighted with plus symbols and dots are used for the other points. It is seen that eight compounds— $CrSi_2$, $CoSb_2$, FeS_2, $OsGe_2$, $ZrGa_2$, $ZrSi_2$, $HfGa_2$ and $TiSi_2$—have very similar orientations, with most of the plus symbols in the second quadrant. The responses to the decision variables of these compounds are also similar, as none of the variable lines are in the second quadrant (Figure 3.5). It is clear from the results how visibly PCA can classify the compounds and find the most suitable structure.

3.4 Problems and Prospects

The concept of data mining is emerging as an important direction for designing new materials. It is fast and can yield practical clues for developing materials with improved performance. This concept can be implemented using statistical techniques as well as CI tools. The aspects of data mining or knowledge discovery using CI tools are dealt with in Chapters 4 through 6. The differences between statistical approaches and CI-based approaches are that the statistical models are simple, transparent and

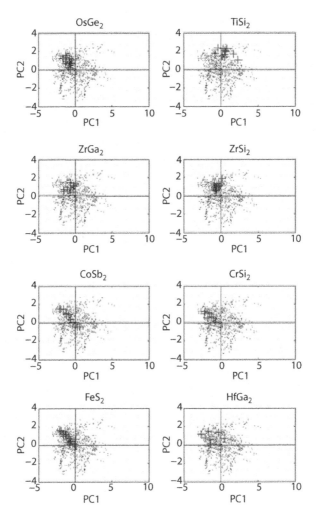

FIGURE 3.4
Some typical results of PCA analysis. (From Agarwal, A. et al. *Materials and Manufacturing Processes* 24: 274–281, 2009. With permission.)

deterministic. This makes things easy to handle. But if the complexity of system is high, this approach shows limitations, primarily due to the inherent structure of these models, which are in many cases linear or pseudolinear in nature. This limitation makes the developed model not applicable for a broad range of variation in the attributes. This issue can be handled by using the models only for the specific ranges for which they are applicable or the range within which the training data actually belonged. But this is generally not mentioned, particularly for models developed earlier and applied for many years. Consider the example of the well-known Hall–Petch equation:

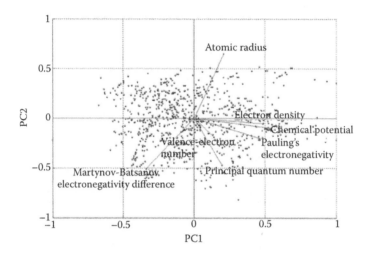

FIGURE 3.5
Score plot for the decision variables. (From Agarwal, A. et al. *Materials and Manufacturing Processes* 24: 274–281, 2009. With permission.)

$\sigma = \sigma_0 + kd^{-1/2}$, where σ is the strength, σ_0 is the friction stress below which the dislocation will not move, k is the stress intensity for transmission of dislocation strain at the grain boundary and d is the grain size. Hall (1951) and Petch (1953) found that the strength varies with $d^{-1/2}$, which they deduced from the data set they used. But Baldwin (1958) showed later that for other materials the variation of strength may be with d^{-1} or even with $d^{-1/3}$. But the Hall–Petch equation is being used without any check for its constraints in applicability. This factor is of utmost importance for using statistical or even other data-driven methods.

References

Agarwal, A., Pettersson, F., Singh, A., Kong, C. S., Saxén, H., Rajan, K., Iwata, S., and Chakraborti, N. 2009. Identification and optimization of AB phases using principal component analysis, evolutionary neural nets, and multiobjective genetic algorithms. *Materials and Manufacturing Processes* 24: 274–281.

Baldwin, W. M. 1958. Yield strength of metals as a function of grain size. *Acta Metallurgica* 6: 139–41.

Bhadeshia, H. K. D. H. 1999. Neural networks in materials science. *ISIJ International* 39: 966–79.

Brieman, L., Friedman, J. H., Olshen, R. A., and Stone, C. J. 1984. *Classification and Regression Trees*. New York: Chapman & Hall.

Chatterjee, S., and Hadi, A. S. 2013. *Regression Analysis by Example*. New Delhi: Wiley India.

Das, P., Bhattacharyay, B. K., and Datta, S. 2006. A comparative study for modeling of hot rolled steel plate classification problem using statistical approach and neural-net systems. *Materials and Manufacturing Processes* 21: 747–55.

Das, P., and Datta, S. 2007. Exploring the effects of chemical composition in hot rolled steel product using Mahalanobis distance scale under Mahalanobis–Taguchi system. *Computational Materials Science* 38: 671–77.

Everitt, B. S., Landau, S., and Leese, M. 2001. *Cluster Analysis*. London: Hodder Arnold.

Gorni, A. A. 2009. *Steel Forming and Heat Treating Handbook*. Brazil. http://www.gorni.eng.br/e/Gorni_SFHTHandbook.pdf (Accessed 11 March 2016).

Grange, R. A. 1961. Estimating critical ranges in heat treatment of steels. *Metal Progress* 70: 73–75.

Hall, E. O. 1951. The deformation and ageing of mild steel: Discussion of results. *Proceedings of the Physical Society of London B* 64: 747–53.

Johnson, R. A., and Wichern, D. W. 1982. *Applied Multivariate Analysis*. Englewood Cliffs, NJ: Prentice Hall.

Liu, H., and Motoda, H. 2007. *Computational Methods of Feature Selection*. Boca Raton, FL: CRC Press.

Mahalanobis, P. C. 1936. On the generalized distance in statistics. *Proceedings of the National Institute of Science of India* 2: 49–55.

Petch, N. J. 1953. The cleavage strength of polycrystals. *The Journal of the Iron and Steel Institute* 174: 25–28.

Rajan, K. 2005. Materials informatics. *Materials Today* 8: 38–45.

Rencher, A. C. 2002. *Methods of Multivariate Analysis*. Hoboken, NJ: John Wiley & Sons.

Suh, C., Rajagopalan, A., Li, X., and Rajan, K. 2002. The application of principal component analysis to materials science data. *Data Science Journal* 1: 19–26.

Taguchi, G., and Jugulum, R. 2002. *The Mahalanobis–Taguchi Strategy: A Pattern Technology System*. New York: John Wiley & Sons.

Vittal, P. R., and Malini, V. 2012. *Statistical and Numerical Methods*. Chennai: Margham.

4

Neural Networks and Genetic Programming for Materials Modelling

The discussion of data-driven techniques of modelling started in Chapter 3, where the statistical tools are discussed in brief. In this chapter we describe two computational intelligence (CI) techniques: artificial neural networks and genetic programming for empirical modelling, which have drawn significant applications in the field of materials modelling. As discussed in Chapter 3, the paradigm of such empirical modelling has shifted from its conventional approach of merely developing a predictive model to knowledge discovery using the data mining concept. In this perspective the CI-based tools have immense importance in modelling materials data, owing to their ability to capture the pattern of highly complex systems from the data. Techniques other than the two dealt with in this chapter, such as support vector machines, are also gradually gaining ground in the materials field. Another facet of data-driven modelling is rule-based modelling, where the rules are extracted from the data. This aspect is discussed in Chapter 5.

4.1 Artificial Neural Networks

Among the CI techniques, the most popular tool in the materials field is the artificial neural network (ANN). ANN basically develops empirical models from experimental or industrial data. In the field of materials engineering, application of statistical regression analysis has been a long tradition for several metallurgical processes, which are discussed in brief in Chapter 3. But ANN became more acceptable since about the mid-1980s because of its flexibility and capability to handle nonlinear systems. The ANN approach of materials modelling is fundamentally different from statistical or numerical methods. ANN does not need any predefined mathematical form, as it learns from examples and recognises patterns of input and output values without any assumptions about their nature (Anderson 1995; Kumar 2004). This inherent flexibility is the main strength of ANN for discovering more complex relationships in data compared with the traditional methods. Several extensive review articles have been published on ANN applications in the materials field (Bhadeshia 1999; Zhang and Friedrich 2003; Datta and Chattopadhyay 2013). The volume of work made by several researchers for developing correlations among the variables from data shows the efficacy of the tool in materials engineering. ANN has been used by researchers for developing empirical models for simulation studies, for finding the optimum range of independent variables to improve the performance of materials, for mining data to find the inherent role of the variables, or even for developing objective functions for optimisation studies. Though fuzzy logic has been extensively employed in different industrial products, processes and control, ANN is the most widely used CI tool in the materials industry, particularly in the steel sector.

ANN is an information processing system inspired by the way biological nervous systems process the information. It is composed of a large number of highly interconnected processing elements, known as neurons, working in unison, designated as a node, processing element or perceptron. The neurons interact with each other through connection strength or weight. ANN is configured for problems such as pattern recognition, data classification or prediction through training or learning processes. Learning in biological systems involves adjustment to the synaptic connections that exist between the neurons. The process of adjusting connection weights with the objective of getting a better response or reducing the prediction error is called learning or training. The process of learning can be supervised or unsupervised depending on the information. In the case of materials, modelling ANN with supervised learning is generally used. Those neural networks are structurally multilayered perceptron, and the prediction error is backpropagated for adjusting the weights. The neural networks have a set of processing units that receive inputs from the outside world, which can be referred to appropriately as the 'input units' or 'input nodes' in a layer called the 'input layer'. It has one or more layers of 'hidden' processing units that receive inputs from the input nodes or the hidden nodes of the preceding layer. The set of units that represent the final result of the neural network are called the 'output units' (Anderson 1995), as shown in Figure 4.1.

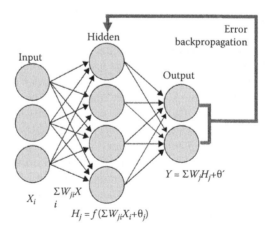

FIGURE 4.1
A typical network structure.

At each hidden unit (H_j), the weighted summation of the inputs (X_i) is operated on by a nonlinear transfer function as shown in Equation 4.1, which ensures that each input contributes to every hidden unit.

$$H_j = f\left(\sum W_{ji}X_i + \theta_j\right) \tag{4.1}$$

The output neuron then calculates a linear weighted sum of the outputs of the hidden units (Equation 4.2).

$$Y = \sum W_j H_j + \theta \tag{4.2}$$

where
Y = output
X_i = normalised inputs
H_j = output from hidden units
W_{ji}, W_j = weights
θ = bias (equivalent to the constant used in regression analysis)

It is thus possible to obtain different outputs by changing the weights and biases. The optimum values of these weights and biases are determined by 'training' the network, which is basically an error minimisation method. For this, the input–output data need to be normalised in the range of –1 to +1, or 0 to +1, depending on the transfer function. A method of normalising between –1 and +1 is shown in Equation 4.3:

$$X_N = \frac{2(X - X_{min})}{X_{max} - X_{min}} - 1 \tag{4.3}$$

where X_N is the normalised value of the input or output variable X and X_{min} and X_{max} are the minimum and maximum values of the variable. The backpropagation algorithm is designed to solve the problem of determining weights and bias values for a multilayered ANN with feed-forward connections from the input layer to the hidden layer(s) and then to the output layer. There are several backpropagation algorithms. The algorithms are iterative and designed to minimise the mean square error between the predicted output and the desired output (Figure 4.2). A more detailed account of backpropagation algorithms can be found in Kumar (2004).

During the learning process certain precautionary measures need to be taken because of the flexibility of the ANN technique and its capability to capture high-level nonlinearity. During training the ANN can capture any bias or peculiarity in the data set and lose the generalisation capability, called overfitting. An overfitted ANN model will predict unknown data poorly. To avoid

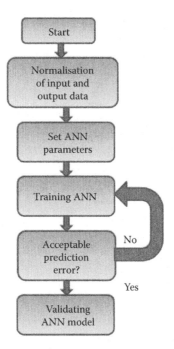

FIGURE 4.2
The scheme for training a neural network.

this problem, the data are divided into two (training and testing) or three (training, testing and validation) parts, where the first part is used for training the model and the other parts for assessing the capacity of the model to predict unknown data. The training error decreases with epochs or iteration of the backpropagation algorithm. The testing or validation error also decreases until overfitting starts, when those errors start increasing. At this exact time the training process is terminated. A typical training curve along with a scatterplot showing the prediction of a trained ANN is shown in Figure 4.3.

On the other hand, unsupervised learning is like learning without a teacher. It does not have any output target. The network discovers patterns, correlations and so forth in the input data. This may be referred to as self-organisation. The outputs in unsupervised networks can be used for familiarity, clustering, feature mapping, and so forth. Unsupervised learning is generally of two types: Hebbian and competitive (Konar 2005). The Hebb Rule is an inherently unsupervised learning rule and can be readily applied. Here the nodes which are active together increase their connection weight, whereas in competitive learning active nodes attempt to inhibit other nodes; the nodes compete and the successful ones prevent the others from firing. Though unsupervised learning has found limited applications in the materials field, there are a few applications of self-organising feature maps,

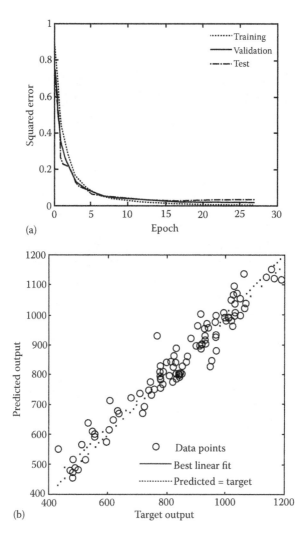

FIGURE 4.3
ANN model behaviour. (a) Error minimisation during training and (b) prediction of outputs after training.

a variant of unsupervised learning. Kohonen (1988) proposed this method of competitive learning. He used a single-layered network and a 'winner takes all' learning rule based on a neighbourhood function, where each node competes to respond to an input vector. The node whose weight vector is closest to that receives the highest net input and wins the competition. This node outputs 1 and all other nodes output 0. Interested readers may refer to Hinton and Sejnowski (1999).

4.2 Genetic Programming

Genetic Programming (GP) was introduced by Koza (1992). As were the other members of the family of evolutionary algorithms, GP was inspired by Darwin's theory of natural selection, and has similarities to its predecessor the Genetic Algorithm (GA), though the general purposes of the two techniques are different. GA is an established optimisation tool, whereas GP is meant for developing a mathematical relationship between the independent and response variables. In GP hierarchically organised mathematical expressions or 'programs' undergo evolution. The size and form of the expressions dynamically change during the process of evolution. The computer programs are represented as treelike structures. Generations after generations evolve through the creation of child computer programs from parent programs. Each individual is in fact a mathematical expression as shown in Figure 4.4. It is also possible to include unary functions such as sine, cosine, tanh, log, and so forth in the function set and a subset of real numbers in the terminal set. A population of individual solutions is initialised by creating a set of random computer programs through the combination of functions with terminals from their respective sets. Each program represents a solution, and a search for the optimum solution in the space of all possible solutions begins. The search is guided by the calculation of 'fitness' of each computer program, which is actually the predictive capacity of the program. Better parents having better fitness are selected with an expectation that they would provide better offspring in the next generation. The GP relation

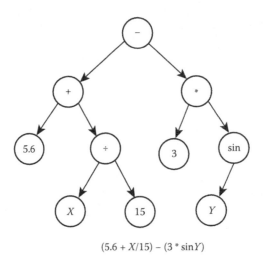

$$(5.6 + X/15) - (3 * \sin Y)$$

FIGURE 4.4
Example of a mathematical expression developed through GP.

evolves through several genetic operators analogously with natural evolution: reproduction, crossover and mutation. This is similar to the GA operators, and is described in detail in Chapter 7. The 'reproduction' operator is a method for preserving the few best individuals that are kept unchanged into the next generation. It is similar to the concept of elitism in GA. The 'crossover' operator effects exchange of genetic material between the programs by grafting branches from one parent onto the stem of the other. 'Mutation' is the change of one node representing a function or a terminal. Finally, a termination criterion is set, which is usually a fixed number of iterations, that determines the point to which the evolutionary iterations are continued.

Depending on the evolved computer program, GP may be utilised to perform different activities, for example, discovering relationships between the variables, selecting the most relevant variables or even deriving rules in a complex data set. However, the most common task, which is utilised in the materials design field, involves finding a nonlinear mathematical relationship between the inputs and the outputs. It may be seen as a generalisation of the statistical linear regression problem, seeking to express the output as just the weighted sum of the inputs.

4.3 Applications in Materials Engineering

As discussed previously, the ANN technique has been explored extensively in the field of materials engineering. The scope and flexibility inherent in the ANN technique inspired its applications in the field of phase transformation, structure–property correlation in alloys, polymers, ceramics, composites, semiconductors, different manufacturing processes including extraction of metals in general and related areas including iron extraction processes, steel making and casting (Datta and Chattopadhyay 2013). In this section a few case studies are discussed to give some idea about handling the tool for a particular purpose.

4.3.1 *In Situ* Prediction of Porosity of Nanostructured Porous Silicon

This is a typical example of an application of ANN in the field of materials design, where the ANN model is developed to predict the porosity of nanostructured silicon (Ray et al. 2008). Silicon, considered the key substrate material in the semiconductor industry, is treated as a potential light emitter, as a consequence of reducing its dimensionality by different techniques. Nanostructured porous silicon (PS) has drawn attention because of its strong room temperature photoluminescence (PL) in the visible region (Canham 1990; Cullis and Canham 1991). However, widespread application of PS could not be achieved owing to the instability and nonuniformity of the structure. The exact mechanism of formation and propagation of pores is still not fully explained yet. Different researchers suggested different mechanisms and proposed different models for the process. But the issue of fabricating PS with an ordered array of nanostructures and uniform pore distribution is not resolved at all, because pore formation in crystalline Si depends on many variables or factors that interact in a complex manner. The most common technique of formation is etching in an HF-based solution, with Si as the anode and a graphite or platinum electrode as the cathode. In this case the parameters that may influence the structure are HF concentration, current density (J) and etching time (t). Surface roughness has a significant impact on pore formation. The effective resistance of the porous layer changes during the process, as the resistivity of the affected portion changes with the growth of pores and formation of the nanostructures which change the voltage drop across the electrodes. Further, the conductivity of the electrolyte inside the pores also varies owing to localised variation of concentration of ions. This in turn results in a local variation of J, which changes the voltage drop across the electrodes. Thus even under a constant current, local current density and resistivity changes are reflected in the fluctuations of the voltage. To handle such complexity in the system, the ANN model is developed to predict porosity on the p-type Si substrate.

For the training of the model a database was generated through laboratory experimentation. PS samples with varying porosities were formed on 2–5 Ω-cm resistivity, p-type (100) orientation crystalline Si wafers by anodisation in an HF–CH$_3$OH solution in a Teflon bath with special electrode geometry. The etching time (t) was varied over a range of 0–30 minutes for five different current densities, J = 5, 10, 15, 20 and 100 mA/cm^2 with a fixed HF concentration of 24% (w/v). Voltage across the electrode was measured at intervals of 5 s for each process.

Figure 4.5 shows that the measured voltage and predicted voltage in different current densities are quite close, and are acceptable for all practical purposes. The findings also clearly indicate that it is possible to develop an ANN model for continuous and *in situ* monitoring of porosity of nanostructured PS. It is also seen that the model predictions are in good agreement with the porosity values obtained by the gravimetric method. The major advantage with the model is that it can be used to predict porosity at any instant during pore formation from the voltage drop across the electrodes, without any destructive method at all. This may be utilised to control the parameters to design the proper structure of the porosity. The model also can be utilised to gain further understanding regarding the relation of the variables with pore size, as seen in Figure 4.6. In this figure the variation of porosity with current density is predicted by the ANN model at different etching times. This type of study can also be utilised to find the suitable combination of parameters to achieve the ideal pore structure.

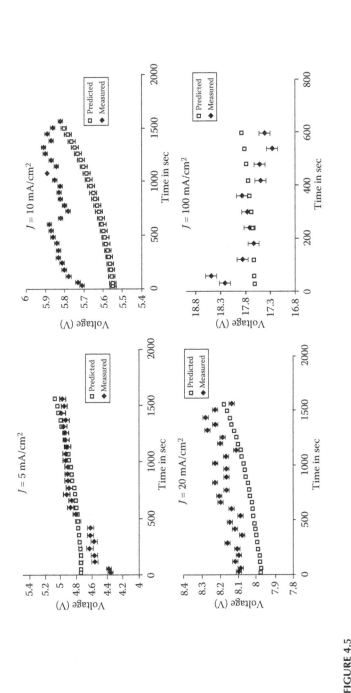

FIGURE 4.5
Comparison of the variation of voltage measured and voltage predicted with time for J = 5, 10, 20 and 100 mA/cm^2. (Reprinted from *Materials and Manufacturing Processes*, 24, Ray, M., Ganguly, S., Das, M., Datta, S., Bandyopadhyay, N. R., and Hossain, S. M. Artificial neural network (ANN)-based model for in situ prediction of porosity of nanostructured porous silicon, pp. 83–87, Copyright 2008, with permission from Taylor & Francis.)

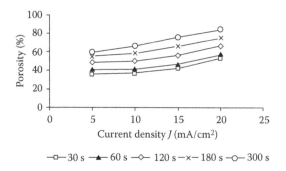

FIGURE 4.6
Variation of porosity with current density for different etching times (t = 30, 60, 120, 180 and 300 s) as predicted by the ANN-based model for a p-Si wafer of resistivity 2–5 Ω-cm. The HF concentration was kept fixed at 24%. (Reprinted from *Materials and Manufacturing Processes*, 24, Ray, M., Ganguly, S., Das, M., Datta, S., Bandyopadhyay, N. R., and Hossain, S. M. Artificial neural network (ANN)-based model for in situ prediction of porosity of nanostructured porous silicon, pp. 83–87, Copyright 2008, with permission from Taylor & Francis.)

4.3.2 Steel Plate Processing

This case study is based on steel processing in industrial situations. Unlike the previous case this problem has a huge number of variables. A considerable problem faced during processing industrial data is that they possess a high amount of noise and uncertainty. Steel plates are produced through plastic deformation using a rolling process. The properties depend on the chemical composition and deformation parameters, as the deformation refines the microstructure and leads to optimum mechanical properties. If the steel is microalloyed it will control the austenite grain growth and in some cases provide precipitation strengthening. Manganese controls the stability of the austenite and thus the nature of the austenite transformation products. The purpose of this work is to develop an ANN model which can estimate strength as a function of a large number of rolling parameters and the chemical composition of the steel, a total of 108 variables (Singh et al. 1998). The data used were obtained directly from an actual plate rolling mill. The input variables are the slab reheating temperature, the length of the slab, the slab gauge, the chemical composition, the rolling parameters and the 'rolling condition' which is set to 0 for rolled plates and 1 for control rolled or normalised rolled plates. The slab reheating temperature determines the initial austenite grain size and the initial temperature of the slab during the rolling process. The timing of the rolling process depends on the length of the slab. The slab gauge is important in determining the total reduction required to achieve the final plate thickness. The chemical composition consists of 14 different elements. The rolling parameters include screw settings of every pass, delay period between the passes and the time spent during each pass.

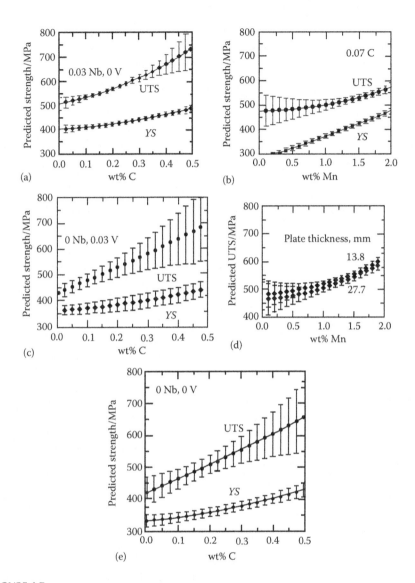

FIGURE 4.7

The role of different variables in varying conditions, as predicted by the ANN model , where (a), (c) and (e) show variation of UTS and YS with wt% C for different levels of Nb and V, and (b) and (d) show variation due to Mn at different levels of C and plate thickness. (Reprinted from *Ironmaking & Steelmaking*, 25, Singh, S. B., Bhadeshia, H. K. D. H., MacKay, D. J. C., Carey, H., and Martin, I. Neural network analysis of steel plate processing, pp. 355–65, Copyright 1998, with permission from Taylor & Francis.)

A neural network model capable of predicting the yield and tensile strengths of steel plates as a function of composition and rolling parameters has been trained and tested. Figure 4.7 consists of a few representative figures showing the effect of different compositional variables (carbon and manganese) on the strength in the presence of different levels of other alloying elements or process parameters. The model has been shown to be consistent with established metallurgical trends and can, for example, be used to study the effect of each variable in isolation. There are interesting results on the yield strength/tensile strength ratio whose value can be altered systematically by controlling the carbon and manganese concentrations. These simulation studies, as discussed earlier, could be utilised meticulously to design composition and process parameters to reach the target properties of the steel as closely as possible within the constraint of the particular plate mill.

4.3.3 Strength of HSLA Steel Using a Customised Network

This case study also relates to developing predictive models for mechanical properties of a high-strength low-alloy (HSLA) grade of steel using ANN (Datta and Banerjee 2006). But here the ANN tool is used in a unique way to incorporate some system knowledge in ANN with a modified architecture. HSLA steel is sometimes subjected to thermomechanical controlled processing (TMCP) for enhancement of mechanical properties. The complicated architecture of the customised network with selective connectivity is constructed as per the physical metallurgy principles. The database comprising the chemical composition and the TMCP parameters (viz. slab reheating temperature, deformation given in three different temperature zones, finish rolling temperature and cooling rate) are used as the input variables and the yield strength is taken as the output variable.

The architecture is constructed in such a way that there are six hidden nodes representing six strengthening mechanisms operative in HSLA steels. They are solid solution hardening, precipitation hardening, dislocation hardening, grain refinement, microstructural modifications and texture hardening (Figure 4.8). All the input variables are connected to six nodes selectively in accordance with the role of the concerned input variable in the strengthening mechanism. As no bias is used, and the network has a hyperbolic tangent as the transfer function, it may be written

$$h_n(k) = \tanh\left\{\sum IW_{n,m}\, p_m(k)\right\} \qquad (4.4)$$

where $h_n(k)$ are the hidden node values generated from the summation of the weighted inputs p, and $IW_{n,m}$ is the input weight. Here n (= 1 to 6) corresponds to the nodes and m is within 1 to 23 corresponding to the inputs. The

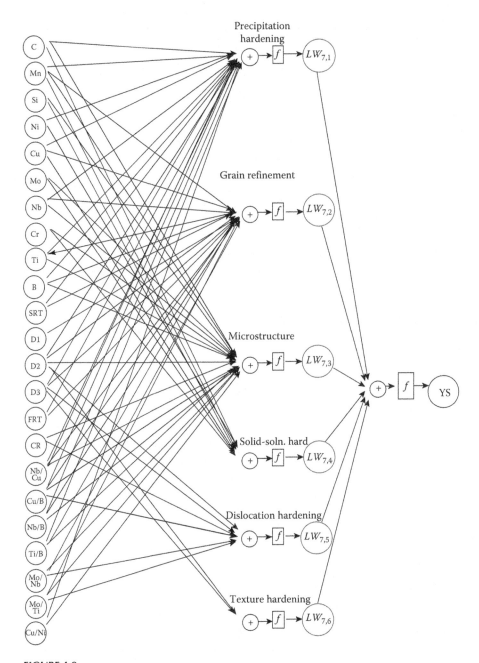

FIGURE 4.8
The structure of the customised ANN. (Reprinted from *Materials Science and Engineering A*, 420, Datta, S., and Banerjee, M. K. Mapping the input output relationship in HSLA steels through expert neural network, pp. 254–64, Copyright 2006, with permission from Elsevier.)

hidden node values are multiplied by the layer weights (*LW*) to get the final output (yield strength) value. This operation can be written as

$$YS = \sum_{n=1}^{6} LW_{6,n} h_n. \tag{4.5}$$

The layer weights, after training, show that the contributions from precipitation hardening, grain refinement, microstructural changes, solid solution hardening and dislocation hardening are high, and the effect of texture hardening is low. Similarly the input weights show that silicon and manganese have the highest and nickel has the lowest contribution to solid solution hardening. When similar plots were developed for the effects of input variables on the dislocation strengthening mechanism, they showed that the combined effect of copper and boron has a maximum contribution towards this mechanism, whereas the combined effect of molybdenum and titanium has the least. In this way the effect of other variables on other strengthening mechanisms are identified comparatively. It is to be noted here that the complex connectivity has enabled the learning process to attain a reasonable degree of accuracy in the prediction of outputs and also to recognise the pattern of the input–output relationship.

4.3.4 An Example of Unsupervised Learning

As previously mentioned, unsupervised learning in ANN is not explored in the field of materials engineering. Here a rare study of this kind of ANN in the form of the Kohonen network is presented (Datta and Banerjee 2004). As in the case of the previous study, here also the properties of HSLA steel in the TMCP condition are modeled through the Self-Organising Map (SOM) or Kohonen network. In the case of data-driven modelling the knowledge base is expressed through the database, which is generally uncertain and not free from error and bias. Automatic estimation of the data by unsupervised learning is one of the methods to overcome such uncertainty.

A remarkable improvement in strength can be achieved in HSLA steel if boron is added in combination with niobium. Combined addition of titanium with boron also has a similar effect. This effect is due mainly to carbide precipitation and grain refinement. The data supplied to the SOM model are plotted as training vectors according to their initial mapping in the input space. After learning the network with 5000 epochs, the weight vectors of the neurons are found to be distributed in such a way that five different clusters are clearly visible in this map. It is seen that the five clusters are made through differentiating the data as per microalloying elements additions and they are

- Steel with niobium
- Steel with titanium
- Steel with niobium and boron
- Steel with titanium and boron
- Steel with niobium, titanium and boron

Thus the SOM is found to be capable of clustering the steel data according to the alloy additions. There should have been more applications of such models in the materials field, as materials engineers deal with data with uncertainty. This type of approach can even be utilised for clustering to detect the cause of poor quality production or defective productions.

4.3.5 Example of an Application of Genetic Programming

Genetic Programming (GP), as already discussed, is another CI-based data-driven modelling tool, which is yet to be explored to its fullest extent in the field of materials engineering. An application of GP on stress distribution during metal forming proposed by Brezocnik et al. (2005) is briefly reported here. Visioplasticity or finite element analysis does not yield exact solutions for real metal-forming problems, as approximations and assumptions exist. To avoid the shortcoming of such models and make the model applicable for practical purposes, the GP technique is employed. Cylindrical specimens of steel are forward extruded with varying coefficients of friction. In the data set thus developed the radial and axial positions of the measured stress node and coefficient of friction are used as the input variables, and radial stress is the output variable. The discrete values of radial stress in each node were obtained by visioplasticity. The data were divided into two groups, the training and testing databases. The GP models thus developed were made to predict the training and testing data sets, and it is seen that the even prediction of the testing data set is quite within acceptable limits (Figure 4.9). The only problem with GP models are their long and complex forms. There are methods to limit the depth of the GP tree and thus reduce the length and complexity of the evolved equation. In such cases the prediction accuracy may be compromised to some extent, but the possibility of overfitting will also be decreased. The beauty of GP models lies in the fact that, unlike the ANN models, they are completely transparent, which provides the additional advantage of understanding the role of the variables. In the case of statistical regression analysis such transparency could be found, but it does not have the flexibility of GP equations. In the case of regression the form of the equation needs to be supplied before, but in GP models the form of the equation evolves. In the process even some of the independent variables may be eliminated, giving the user the scope to find the important variables also.

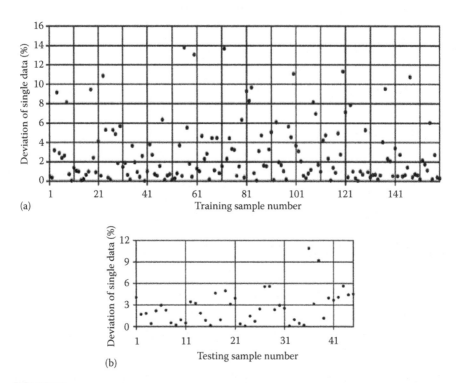

(a)

(b)

FIGURE 4.9
Percentage variation of the predictions made by the GP models for the (a) training data set and
(b) testing dataset. (Reprinted from *Materials and Manufacturing Processes*, 20, Brezocnik, M.,
Kovacic, M., and Gusel, L. Comparison between genetic algorithm and genetic programming
approach for modeling the stress distribution, pp. 497–508, Copyright 2005, with permission
from Taylor & Francis.)

4.4 Suitability as Materials Design Tools

The preceding case studies clearly show that ANN has the capability to
develop a mathematical correlation between input and output variables in
highly complex materials systems. But developing a good model does not
lead to materials design automatically. A good model can be utilised in different ways for searching new compositions or modified processing routes
to achieve improved performance of materials. A neural network model
can be utilised to find the role of the different variables using simulation
studies and also through sensitivity analysis (Dey et al. 2016). This knowledge discovery through data mining along with existing knowledge may be
used for designing new materials. The developed model can be used as the

objective function for an optimisation search. This approach is discussed in Chapter 8. Another approach is systematic simulation using the trained ANN model to find a combination of the input parameters capable of achieving the goal. This approach is discussed in this section with another example of HSLA steel.

Here the goal is to find a suitable combination of copper and microalloying elements along with processing parameters to achieve better tensile properties with and without ageing treatment (Ghosh et al. 2009). When the steel is not subjected to ageing, the variables are similar to the ones before, that is, composition; slab reheating temperature (SRT); three deformation amounts in three temperature regimes D1, D2 and D3; finish rolling temperature (FRT) and cooling rate (CR). For steel with ageing treatment the prestrain and ageing parameters are the additional parameters. The trained model is used for prediction or simulation studies. A chemical composition of (wt%) 0.04 C, 1.58 Mn, 0.47 Si is chosen as the base composition of steel to study the effect of the variations of microalloying elements and Cu to achieve the optimum level of yield ratio (YR). Among the process parameters SRT and FRT were fixed at 1200°C and 750°C respectively and D1, D2 and D3 were set at 24%, 16% and 8% respectively. Two post-rolling cooling rates of 5°C/s and 95°C/s (DQ samples) were considered to represent the direct air cooling (DAC) and direct water quenching (DQ) respectively after completion of rolling.

Figure 4.10 shows the response of the Ti and B addition on the YR for DAC and DQ conditions. The influence of the elements is found to be more prominent in the case of DAC steels. But DQ steels have a higher YR. Ti seems to be more effective in the DAC steels. The concentration ranges of Ti and B – 0.03 0.04 wt% and 0.0025–0.003 wt% respectively – seem to be effective and were chosen for further simulation.

In the selected levels of B and Ti, the effect of Cu addition on the properties of the steel was studied. Figure 4.11 shows that at lower levels of YR, in both DAC and DQ steels, an increase in Cu increases the UTS. The best combinations of YR and % elongation, a desired property combination, is achieved at Cu concentration of around 1.5 wt%. In the case of DQ steels also, a Cu concentration between 1.0 and 1.5 wt% provides the best combination of tensile properties. In this way the level of Cu and microalloying additions are finalised to obtain the best combination of properties through virtual experimentation using trained ANN models.

Steel with a chemical composition (wt%) 0.04 C, 1.69 Mn, 0.57 Si, 0.03 Ti, 0.0013 B is then used as the base alloy to study the effects of Cu, prestrain and ageing parameters when the tensile properties of the steel are measured in the aged condition. Again the design approach of systematic simulation is used to find the effect of ageing parameters and prestrain on ageing kinetics towards maximization of strength and ductility using the knowledge of the model.

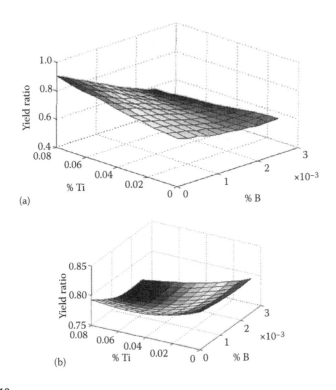

FIGURE 4.10
Surface views of the relations between yield ratio (YR) and % Ti–% B combinations of (a) DAC steel and (b) DQ steel. (Reprinted from *Ironmaking & Steelmaking*, 36, Ghosh, S. K., Ganguly, S., Chattopadhyay, P. P., and Datta, S. Effect of copper and microalloying (Ti, B) addition on tensile properties of HSLA steels predicted by ANN technique, pp. 125–32, Copyright 2009, with permission from Taylor & Francis.)

The influence of Cu addition and ageing temperature on UTS and % elongation is shown in Figure 4.12. It is evident that the strength of the steel is greatly influenced by the amount of Cu added, but marginally by the ageing temperature over the range of Cu concentrations. Cu precipitation seems to have no additional effect on UTS if Cu is added at a concentration greater than 1.5 wt%.

When ageing time is considered, ageing temperature is fixed at 500°C (Figure 4.13). The figure shows that both UTS and elongation values increase with Cu concentration. But ageing time has a detrimental effect on both the properties after 1000 minutes of ageing. The other new processing parameter – prestraining – is now considered. Figure 4.14 shows the influence of prestrain on steel properties, where Cu addition is fixed at 1.5 wt% and ageing duration at 150 minutes. It is apparent that both parameters have a positive effect on the UTS values and the enhancement is most prominent at a higher ageing temperature and % prestrain.

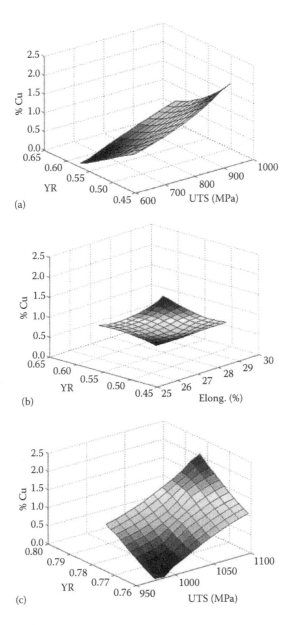

FIGURE 4.11
Surface views of the relations between (a) % Cu and UTS–YR, (b) % Cu and elongation (%)–YR combinations of DAC steels and (c) % Cu and UTS–YR. *(Continued)*

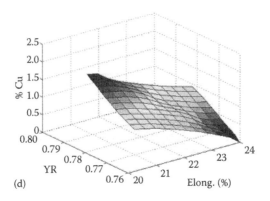

(d)

FIGURE 4.11 (CONTINUED)
Surface views of the relations between (d) % Cu and elongation (%)–YR combinations of DQ steels. (Reprinted from *Ironmaking & Steelmaking*, 36, Ghosh, S. K., Ganguly, S., Chattopadhyay, P. P., and Datta, S. Effect of copper and microalloying (Ti, B) addition on tensile properties of HSLA steels predicted by ANN technique, pp. 125–32, Copyright 2009, with permission from Taylor & Francis.)

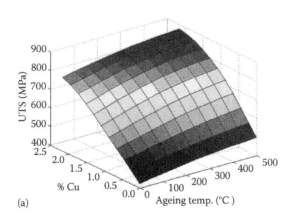

(a)

FIGURE 4.12
Surface views of the relations between (a) UTS and ageing temperature–% Cu.　　(*Continued*)

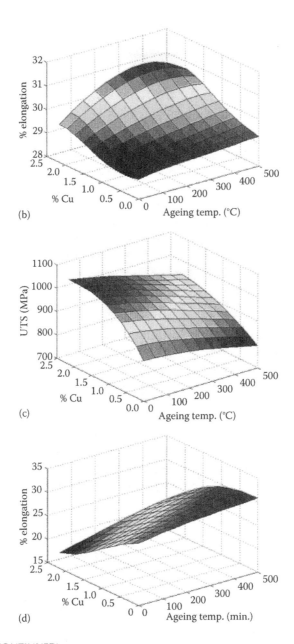

FIGURE 4.12 (CONTINUED)
Surface views of the relations between (b) % elongation and ageing temperature–% Cu combinations of DAC steels, (c) UTS and ageing temperature–% Cu, (d) % elongation and ageing temperature–% Cu combinations of DQ steels. (Reprinted from *Ironmaking & Steelmaking*, 36, Ghosh, S. K., Ganguly, S., Chattopadhyay, P. P., and Datta, S. Effect of copper and microalloying (Ti, B) addition on tensile properties of HSLA steels predicted by ANN technique, pp. 125–32, Copyright 2009, with permission from Taylor & Francis.)

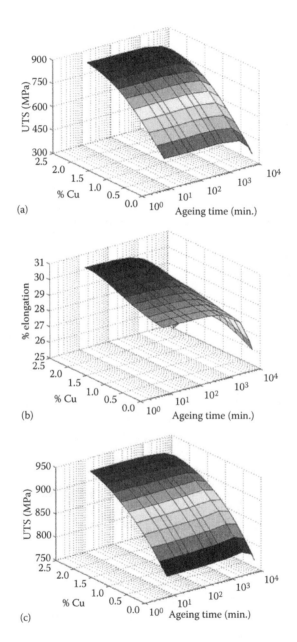

FIGURE 4.13
Surface views of the relations between (a) UTS and ageing time–% Cu, (b) % elongation and ageing time–% Cu combinations of DAC steels, (c) UTS and ageing time–% Cu.   (*Continued*)

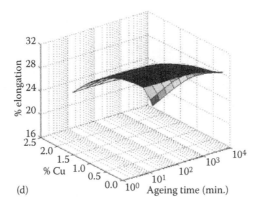

(d)

FIGURE 4.13 (CONTINUED)
Surface views of the relations between (d) % elongation and ageing time–% Cu combinations of DQ steels. (Reprinted from *Ironmaking & Steelmaking*, 36, Ghosh, S. K., Ganguly, S., Chattopadhyay, P. P., and Datta, S. Effect of copper and microalloying (Ti, B) addition on tensile properties of HSLA steels predicted by ANN technique, pp. 125–32, Copyright 2009, with permission from Taylor & Francis.)

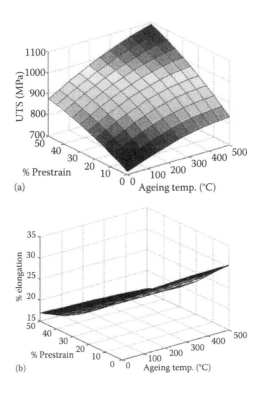

(a)

(b)

FIGURE 4.14
Surface views of the relations between (a) UTS and ageing temperature–% prestrain, (b) % elongation and ageing temperature–% prestrain combinations of DAC steels. *(Continued)*

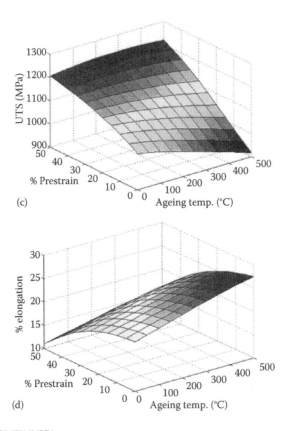

FIGURE 4.14 (CONTINUED)
Surface views of the relations between (c) UTS and ageing temperature–% prestrain and (d) % elongation and ageing temperature–% prestrain combinations of DQ steels. (Reprinted from *Ironmaking & Steelmaking*, 36, Ghosh, S. K., Ganguly, S., Chattopadhyay, P. P., and Datta, S. Effect of copper and microalloying (Ti, B) addition on tensile properties of HSLA steels predicted by ANN technique, pp. 125–32, Copyright 2009, with permission from Taylor & Francis.)

In this way the optimum combination of all the parameters could be found which could give the steel a better property composite. This approach is similar to systematic laboratory experimentation to find the best combination of composition and process parameters to achieve the target. The difference is that the volume of the aforementioned virtual experimentation could be completed in only months of experimentation in real life, thus saving time and money. But the most important point is that a reliable model needs to be developed first; otherwise such predictions will lead nowhere.

References

Anderson, J. A. 1995. *An Introduction to Neural Networks*. Cambridge, MA: MIT Press.

Bhadeshia, H. K. D. H. 1999. Neural networks in materials science. *ISIJ International* 39: 966–79.

Brezocnik, M., Kovacic, M., and Gusel, L. 2005. Comparison between genetic algorithm and genetic programming approach for modeling the stress distribution. *Materials and Manufacturing Processes* 20: 497–508.

Canham, L. T. 1990. Silicon quantum wire array fabrication by electrochemical and chemical dissolution of wafers. *Applied Physics Letters* 57: 1045–48.

Cullis, A. G., and Canham, L. T. 1991. Visible light emission due to quantum size effects in highly porous crystalline silicon. *Nature* 353: 335–38.

Datta, S., and Banerjee, M. K. 2004. Kohonen network modeling of thermo-mechanically processed HSLA steel. *ISIJ International* 44: 846–51.

Datta, S., and Banerjee, M. K. 2006. Mapping the input output relationship in HSLA steels through expert neural network. *Materials Science and Engineering A* 420: 254–64.

Datta, S., and Chattopadhyay, P. P. 2013. Soft computing techniques in advancement of structural metals. *International Materials Reviews* 58: 475–504.

Dey, S., Sultana, N., Kaiser, S. M., and Datta, S. 2016. Computational intelligence based design of age-hardenable aluminium alloy for different temperature regime. *Materials and Design* 92: 522–34.

Ghosh, S. K., Ganguly, S., Chattopadhyay, P. P., and Datta, S. 2009. Effect of copper and microalloying (Ti, B) addition on tensile properties of HSLA steels predicted by ANN technique. *Ironmaking and Steelmaking* 36: 125–32.

Hinton, G., and Sejnowski, T. J. eds. 1999. *Unsupervised Learning: Foundations of Neural Computation*. Cambridge, MA: MIT Press.

Kohonen, T. 1988. *Self-Organizing and Associative Memory*. Berlin: Springer-Verlag.

Konar, A. 2005. *Computational Intelligence*. Berlin: Springer-Verlag.

Koza, J. R. 1992. *Genetic Programming: On the Programming of Computers by Means of Natural Selection*. Cambridge, MA: MIT Press.

Kumar, S. 2004. *Neural Networks-A Classroom Approach*. New Delhi: Tata McGraw-Hill.

Ray, M., Ganguly, S., Das, M., Datta, S., Bandyopadhyay, N. R., and Hossain, S. M. 2008. Artificial neural network (ANN)-based model for in situ prediction of porosity of nanostructured porous silicon. *Materials and Manufacturing Processes* 24: 83–87.

Singh, S. B., Bhadeshia, H. K. D. H., MacKay, D. J. C., Carey, H., and Martin, I. 1998. Neural network analysis of steel plate processing, *Ironmaking and Steelmaking* 25: 355–65.

Zhang, Z., and Friedrich, K. 2003. Artificial neural networks applied to polymer composites: A review. *Composites Science and Technology* 63: 2029–44.

5

Knowledge Extraction Using Fuzzy and Rough Set Theories

Some of the tools, both statistics and computational intelligence (CI) based, for data-driven modelling and knowledge discovery from data with their applications in the materials design domain, were discussed in Chapters 3 and 4. But the mappings of the inputs to the output space, using those tools, are either linear or pseudo-linear in nature, or too complex to be perceivable, or require a black box to be inserted between the input and output spaces. Fuzzy logic can provide a superior approach, as the fuzzy system is faster, less expensive and conceptually easier to understand. It is capable of modelling nonlinear arbitrary relationships, highly tolerant of imprecise data, and the most important advantage of analysing data using fuzzy logic is that it could be used for developing linguistic if–then rules to describe the correlation between the predictor variables or the inputs and the response variables or the outputs, making the knowledge inherent in the system easy to understand. In this chapter, methods of extraction of fuzzy if–then rules from data are described after a brief portrayal of the principle of fuzzy logic. Some examples of applications of such rule extraction practice and consequent development of fuzzy models in the materials field are studied also. In the case of data processing, feature selection or finding the important variables in a system is an important task. Rough set theory has the capacity to find the important attributes or variables of a system from the data. Here the data are first analysed to assess relative importance of the parameters, and then the rules are derived using a minimum number of attributes. In both approaches – fuzzy set and rough set theories – finally a set of rules could be extracted from the given data set, which makes the information and knowledge expressed in the rule easy to interpret. These rules then can be utilised to form a fuzzy inference system (FIS), which is simply a modelling concept having an input–output correlation. Even existing imprecise knowledge, if expressed in the form of if–then rules, can also be used for generating an FIS, which is discussed in Chapter 6.

5.1 Fuzzy Logic

Fuzzy logic may be expressed as a superset of conventional (Boolean) logic, suitable for handling the uncertainty in data and imprecision in knowledge. Dr. Lotfi Zadeh introduced the concept in 1960s (Zadeh 1965). Subsequently, the application area expanded over a wide spectrum ranging from consumer products and electronic instruments to automobile and traffic monitoring systems. It can be used in trading off between significance and precision. A fuzzy set is a set without a crisp or clearly defined boundary. The set contains elements with only a degree of membership; as in fuzzy logic the truth of any statement becomes a matter of degree. The membership value (or degree of membership) of each point in the input space is mapped to a value between 0 and 1 by a membership function (MF), which is a curve whose shape can be defined as a function that is suitable in terms of simplicity, convenience, speed and efficiency (Figure 5.1). The simplest membership functions are formed using straight lines. Among these, the triangular and trapezoidal membership functions are most common.

An FIS has three components: (1) the fuzzifier, (2) the inference engine with fuzzy rule base and (3) the defuzzifier (Ganesh 2006). The purpose of fuzzification is to map the inputs to values from 0 to 1 using a set of input membership functions. Fuzzy rules are employed to develop the fuzzy outputs of different rules. The outputs are then combined to obtain one fuzzy output distribution. There are several methods of obtaining fuzzy combinations, which are not discussed here. Fuzzy combinations are generally referred to as 'T-norms'. In many instances, it is desired to come up with a single crisp output from an FIS. This crisp number is obtained in a process known as defuzzification. There are several techniques for defuzzifying. The process is described schematically in Figure 5.2.

Two most common types of FISs are the Mamdani (Mamdani and Assilian 1975) and the Sugeno (Sugeno 1977) FISs. The primary difference is that in the Sugeno FIS there is no output membership function at all. Here the

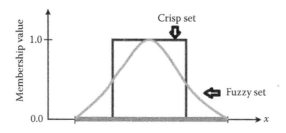

FIGURE 5.1
Membership functions of crisp and fuzzy sets.

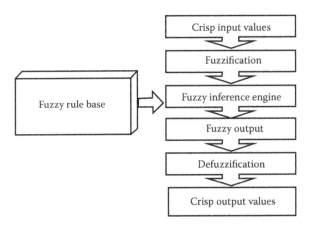

FIGURE 5.2
A schematic representation of FIS.

output is a crisp number calculated by multiplying each input by a constant and then adding up. As evident from the preceding discussion, FIS is suitable for modelling systems where on one hand the imprecise knowledge is expressed in a linguistic if–then rule manner rather than by mathematical expression, and on the other hand data are not available for developing data-driven models such as artificial neural networks. A more detailed account of FIS is provided in Chapter 6.

5.1.1 Rule Extraction Using Clustering Methods

A cluster can be defined as a group of objects that are more similar to one another than to members of other clusters. Most of the clustering techniques divide or organise data into groups. The concept of clustering is unsupervised, which means the user does not provide to the algorithm the target groups where the data need to be clustered. The algorithm itself finds the clusters based on the similarities among the data set. This potential of clustering the algorithm is used in a range of applications, including classification, image processing, pattern recognition, modelling and identification. As clusters are subsets of the data set, clustering methods can be fuzzy or crisp. As evident, the crisp clustering methods are based on classical set theory, which states that an object either belongs to a cluster or does not, that is, it has a membership value of either 1 or 0 in a particular cluster. Fuzzy clustering methods allow the objects to belong to several clusters simultaneously, with varying degrees of membership, between 0 and 1. There are different fuzzy clustering algorithms; among them, the fuzzy c-means algorithm is most familiar. In this clustering method, any point x in the data set has a set of coefficients giving its degree of membership in any cluster. With fuzzy c-means, the centroid of a cluster is the weighted arithmetic mean of all points, where the weight is the membership value. Thus the centroid is calculated in an iterative manner as

$$C_p = \frac{\sum w_p x}{\sum w_p}.$$

The degree of membership, w_p, is related inversely to the distance from x to the cluster center as calculated on the previous pass. Each cluster identifies a region in the data space that contains a sufficient number of data to form a fuzzy input–output relationship (Chiu 1997). A rule can be generated only where there is a cluster of data. This approach of rule extraction helps avoid the formation of a huge number of rules. Thus extracting fuzzy rules is actually partitioning the input space into appropriate fuzzy sets or clusters. The methods of extraction finally bank on some kind of iterative searching algorithm for a base set of rules to describe the system. It may be unsupervised, in which the algorithm finalises the number of clusters or number of membership functions to divide one attribute. Other than c-means clustering, other clustering methods such as complete link clustering or even the grid partitioning method may be employed. In the case of supervised training, an optimisation algorithm is employed to search the rule for a given set of fuzzy clusters. The optimisation method may be evolutionary algorithms with single or multiple objectives. Evolutionary fuzzy systems arguably have a better capability to find the best set of rules and the structures of the fuzzy systems. Multiobjective optimisation techniques can be utilised to achieve the conflicting objective of high prediction accuracy of the developed FIS and simplicity of the fuzzy rules for better interpretability of the fuzzy systems (Zhang and Mahfouf 2008). These types of approaches also have the flexibility to develop Mamdani type fuzzy models using evolutionary algorithms, and thus are becoming more and more accepted for extracting rules and developing fuzzy models from a database.

5.2 Rough Set Theory

Rough Set Theory (RST), proposed by Pawlak (1982), is a generalisation of the classical set theory. The theory is derived from the logical properties of information systems and can be described as a methodology of data mining or knowledge discovery. RST also deals with uncertainty mathematics such as the fuzzy theory. RST extends the concept of well-defined sets by considering the existence of elements that neither 'belong' nor 'do not belong' to a particular set, forming a grey region where the element 'probably belongs'. RST has the important capacity to reduce a data table by eliminating redundant information and selecting the important features. The difference between rough and fuzzy sets lies in the approach of dealing with imprecision, where fuzzy sets describes it for partial memberships and RST defines it for multiple memberships. RST assumes that every object associated with some information, and objects carrying the same information, are indiscernible (similar). In a data set or information system the rows represent objects and columns represent attributes (properties). For any information system $I = (U, A)$ consisting of U objects for a set of attributes A, it is possible to describe the system through $X \subseteq U$ using only the information in $B \subseteq A$ by defining the B-lower and B-upper approximations of X, denoted by $\underline{B}X$ and $\overline{B}X$, respectively (Figure 5.3).

If the quantitative experimental data of an object are expressed with some tolerance, within a numerical range or even in a qualitative way, the entire range of attribute values may be divided into smaller intervals, called discretisation. The intervals may be described linguistically as 'low', 'medium' or 'high' or in some qualitative measure. This reduces the number of attributes and makes the system simple and comprehendible without losing important information. After discretisation, the duplicate objects are eliminated, leading to a new form of attribute combinations. The reduct of an information system is the minimal subset of the conditional attributes (or the input variables) using the same decisions. Various methods are available to find the reducts (Dey et al. 2009). In this process rough sets identify the significant variables in a complex system having a large amount of variables. The numerical and/or categorical information is then converted to rules, into a form that is understood by human users, to make it easy to interpret the information. The rule extraction algorithms deal with the reduced information system and express them as decision rules.

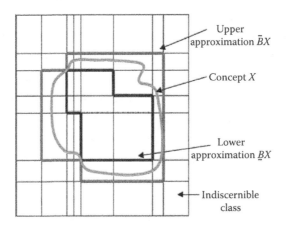

FIGURE 5.3
Approximation of concepts in Rough Set Theory. (Reprinted from *Materials and Manufacturing Processes*, 24, Dey, S., Dey, P., Datta, S., and Sil, J. Rough set approach to predict the strength and ductility of TRIP steel, pp. 150–54. Copyright 2009, with permission from Taylor & Francis.)

5.3 Case Studies of Successful Applications

The preceding discussion looked at the fact that both fuzzy and rough sets could be used for the purposes of rule extraction from data in the direction of knowledge discovery and also for developing predictive models using the rules. Most of the utilities are highly applicable in the field of materials modelling and design, as large amounts of data are being generated in materials systems using so many characterisation techniques. This section provides a brief overview of the applications of these two concepts in the materials field.

5.3.1 Friction Stir Welding of Al Alloys

A fuzzy model for friction stir welding (FSW) of an Al–Mg alloy (AA5083) was developed using experimental data (Zhang et al. 2011). Here multiobjective optimization was adopted to extract the rules. Two independent variables, tool rotation speed (RS) (rpm) in a clockwise or counterclockwise direction and forward movement per revolution (FM) (mm/rev) along the line of joint, control the FSW process. A higher tool rotation speed means a higher temperature due to higher friction. Experimentally the welding is done using five different rotation speeds between 200 and 600 rpm and five different forward movement rates of 0.6, 0.8, 1.0, 1.2 and 1.4 mm/rev. The first model was developed to predict the yield strength (YS), ultimate tensile strength (UTS), reduction of area (ROA), and elongation at room temperature. Tensile testing is conducted with the nugget zone in transverse orientation to the weld, as it represents the weakest direction in FSW. During testing it was seen that failures occurred mainly as shear fractures in the heat-affected zone (HAZ), because the HAZ has the lowest strength as a result of coarsening of precipitates and development of precipitate-free zones (PFZs). It can also be assumed that failures may occur in the nugget zones due to the presence of voids and other defects.

Several models were developed using different sets of rules extracted from the experimental data of tensile properties. It is seen that the predictability decreased with a decreasing number of rules. But it is easy to understand the inherent relations between the variables of a system using a fewer number of rules. The sets of rules having minimum rules are described below (Zhang et al. 2011).

1. If (RS is medium small) and (FM is medium large), then (YS is small).
2. If (RS is small) and (FM is large), then (YS is large).
3. If (RS is large) and (FM is small), then (YS is small).
4. If (RS is large) and (FM is medium), then (YS is medium).

It was also observed through simulation studies using the models that, though there are certain differences in capturing the role of the variables in these two models, for all practical purposes the model with fewer rules is quite acceptable. With regard to friction stir weld quality, the common defects faced are porosity and surface defects. To evaluate quality, a bend test, surface inspection, and cross section inspection were carried out. Based on these tests, an overall weld quality index (WQ) was calculated. In this case also it is seen that more rules lead to greater accuracy, but with fewer rules the system becomes easier to interpret. The following are the rules for welding quality (Zhang et al. 2011):

1. If (RS is medium) and (FM is large), then (WQ is medium small).
2. If (RS is medium large) and (FM is medium small), then (WQ is small).
3. If (RS is very large) and (FM is small), then (WQ is medium small).
4. If (RS is very large) and (FM is large), then (WQ is large).

The method of extraction of fuzzy if–then rules from experimental data and developing predictive fuzzy models using those rules was found to provide both adequate predictability and a transparent interpretable model to extract knowledge from the data. This is the most significant advantage of fuzzy modelling. But readers should be aware of one negative aspect of this type of modelling: the issue of handling a large number of variables. In such a situation the interpretability of the fuzzy rules declines as the complexity of the system increases. The requirement of fuzzy rules also increases the possibility to achieve sufficient predictability. This aspect could better be handled by rough set theory, owing to its capacity to reduce the number of variables. Such an application in materials domain is described later. Another approach to handling a complicated system with a larger number of variables with fuzzy models itself is described in the next section.

5.3.2 Ultrasonic Drilling of Ceramic Materials

This is another example of fuzzy rule extraction from experimental data. The only difference from the previous case is that the rules are generated for the Sugeno type FIS, where a conventional derivative-based optimization algorithm is applied, and thus fall under the broad category of neuro-fuzzy inference system. Ultrasonic machining (USM) is applied mostly for the machining of nonconductive, brittle materials such as engineering ceramics. The specialty of this type of machining process is nonthermal and nonchemical, and it does not generate any change in the microstructure. In the present work penetration time and penetration depth are the inputs, and material removal rate of the machining process acts as the output (Singh and Gill 2009). The Sugeno-type fuzzy interface system, used in this work, can map the relation between the input and output data through a learning process similar to an artificial neural network to determine the optimal distribution of membership functions. The basic structure of the Sugeno type inference system is shown in Figure 5.4. As mentioned in Section 5.1, in the case of the Sugeno type FIS the output depends on a weighted summation of the inputs. In the case of two inputs, x and y, and one output f in the FIS, the fuzzy if–then rules will be as follows:

Rule 1: If x is A_1 and y is B_1, then $f = p_1x + q_1y + r_1$.
Rule 2: If x is A_2 and y is B_2, then $f = p_2x + q_2y + r_2$.

In the process of fuzzy clustering of the present data set, four membership functions were generated for each input variables. The output variable also contained four membership functions. The major drawback of this type of FIS is the lack of transparency, as the output membership functions do not clearly signify any level and the rules becomes less comprehendible. A discrepancy in results, as depicted in Figure 5.5, is another shortcoming of this process. As the rule generation and the final learning process from data depend on gradient-based optimization, there is every possibility of getting stuck in a local optima. In such cases the learning will be different even if the same process is repeated. Such a difference has appeared in the case of the surface views of Figure 5.5a and b. Simulation studies on the variation of the inputs show a different nature of variation in the output.

Though the Sugeno type FIS has certain disadvantages, as discussed previously, it is still the most popular method of fuzzy rule extraction from data owing to its neural network–like approach. Figure 5.6 shows the efficacy of such rules in controlling any manufacturing process precisely, as the FIS developed in this process can achieve a high level of accuracy in prediction.

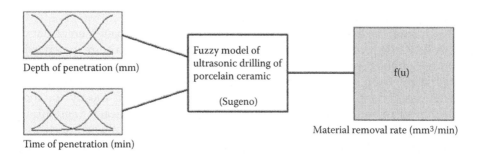

FIGURE 5.4
Structure of the fuzzy model for ultrasonic drilling. (Reprinted from *Materials and Manufacturing Processes*, 24, Singh, J., and Gill, S. S. Fuzzy modeling and simulation of ultrasonic drilling of porcelain ceramic with hollow stainless steel tools, pp. 468–75, Copyright 2009, with permission from Taylor & Francis.)

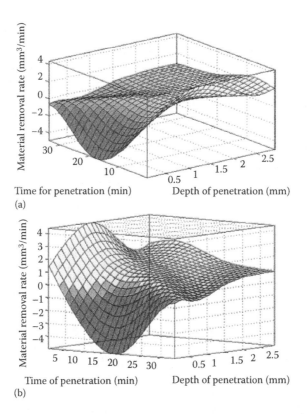

FIGURE 5.5
Surface views generated from the neuro-fuzzy models for different training or error minimi-
zation steps. (Reprinted from *Materials and Manufacturing Processes*, 24, Singh, J., and Gill, S. S.
Fuzzy modeling and simulation of ultrasonic drilling of porcelain ceramic with hollow stainless steel tools, pp. 468–75, Copyright 2009, with permission from Taylor & Francis.)

5.3.3 Mechanical Properties of Ti Alloys

In this work both fuzzy rules from existing imprecise knowledge and fuzzy
rules from experimental data are utilised to develop an FIS of complex structure (Datta et al. 2016). The approach of developing models using expert
knowledge in the form of imprecise linguistic rules is discussed in Chapter 6.
Hence here the methodology of developing the rule-based model from system
knowledge will not be discussed. How the rules developed from prior knowledge and the rules developed from data could be used together is shown here.
Among the metallic biomaterials, suitable for replacing failed hard tissues,
titanium alloys are drawing the greatest attention owing to excellent specific
strength and the best biocompatibility. Though pure titanium and Ti–6Al–4V
still are being used for the purpose owing to their easy availability, β-type titanium alloys are advantageous from the aspect of mechanical biocompatibility
owing to their lower elastic modulus. This property is regarded as an important

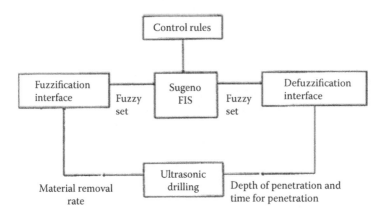

FIGURE 5.6
Controlling the ultrasonic drilling system using fuzzy rules. (Reprinted from *Materials and Manufacturing Processes*, 24, Singh, J., and Gill, S. S. Fuzzy modeling and simulation of ultrasonic drilling of porcelain ceramic with hollow stainless steel tools, pp. 468–75, Copyright 2009, with permission from Taylor & Francis.)

factor, as a low elastic modulus reduces stress shielding of the neighbouring bone (Hin 2004). But pure Ti and $\alpha + \beta$ type Ti–6Al–4V alloys have an elastic modulus of 105–110 GPa, while human cortical bone has a stiffness of around 20 GPa. The published experimental data are collected from various sources to develop a predictive fuzzy model to design a new Ti alloy having low elastic modulus but adequate strength, the best combination of properties required for orthopedic implant. The input variables consist of compositional variables and processing parameters and the output variables are the elastic modulus and yield strength. A two-layered fuzzy inference system is developed, in which the input variables in the first layer are related to six microstructural features important for determining the mechanical properties, and the six features are then connected to the properties in the second layer (Figure 5.7). Six Mamdani FISs correlating the composition and process variables with microstructural features are developed using prior knowledge of the system. Two Mamdani FISs correlating the microstructural features with the properties is developed using the database generated from the published literature.

The six FISs describing the microstructural features are (1) volume fraction of β, (2) solid solution hardening, (3) grain size, (4) acicularity, (5) defects in the microstructure and (6) other decomposition products. The details of rule development in this part are beyond the scope of this chapter but can be found in Datta et al. (2016). The rule bases for the second part of the model are generated separately using the database. Here also the rules are evolved using error minimisation for predicting the existing database using all possible rule sets. The Reduced Space Searching Algorithm (RSSA; Zhang and Mahfouf 2010), a nature-inspired search technique which aims to shift the search space to a subspace including the 'optimum', is used here for error minimisation.

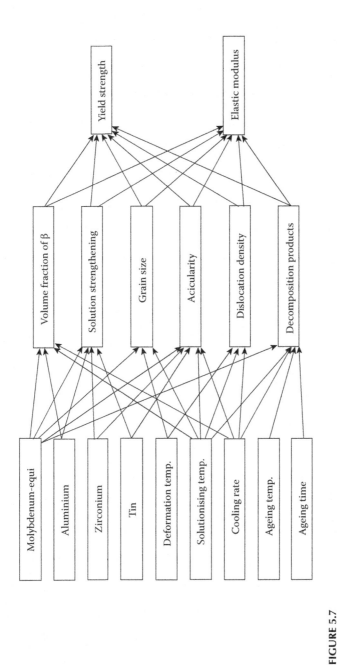

FIGURE 5.7

Schematic of the fuzzy model. (Reprinted from *Journal of Mechanical Behavior of Biomedical Materials*, 53, Datta, S., Mahfouf, M., Zhang, Q., Chattopadhyay, P. P., and Sultana, N. 2016. Imprecise knowledge based design and development of titanium alloys for prosthetic applications, pp. 350–65. Copyright 2016, with permission from Elsevier.)

The following are a few rules relating the microstructural features and the YS for Ti alloys, generated from the minimisation of the error for predicting the existing database (Datta et al. 2016):

1. If (volume fraction of β is low) and (solution hardening is low) and (grain size is low) and (acicularity is high) and (dislocation density is high) and (decomposition product is low) then (YS is high).

2. If (volume fraction of β is low) and (solution hardening is medium) and (grain size is medium) and (dislocation density is high) and (decomposition product is medium) then (YS is high).

3. If (solution hardening is medium) and (grain size is low) and (acicularity is high) and (dislocation density is high) and (decomposition product is medium) then (YS is medium).

The total number of rules was 15, and the high number of rules indicates the complexity of the system. As we have previously discussed, a higher number of rules makes the model less transparent and the purpose of extracting fuzzy rules is lost. But when one is dealing with a complex system and trying to reveal the effect of microstructural features on the final property, the options become limited. A lower number of rules in this case could have improved the interpretability, but with a huge compromise in predictability. The predictions made by the YS model are shown in Figure 5.8. The response surfaces generated by the model are shown in Figure 5.9. The figures reveal that the effect of the volume fraction of β has been significant, but that of grain size is not. In the case of a solid solution, hardening due to addition of alloying elements, the strength increases initially, then drops. The effect of precipitation of the other decomposition products is not high at higher solute content, where presumably the microstructure is predominantly β.

A few rules for the other model (elastic modulus) are described as follows (Datta et al. 2016):

1. If (volume fraction of β is low) and (solution hardening is medium) and (grain size is low) and (acicularity is medium) and (dislocation density is high) and (decomposition product is high) then (elastic modulus is low).

2. If (solution strength is high) and (grain size is medium) and (acicularity is high) and (dislocation density is low) and (decomposition product is low) then (elastic modulus is medium).

3. If (volume fraction of β is high) and (solution hardening is low) and (grain size is low) and (acicularity is high) and (dislocation density is low) and (decomposition product is low) then (elastic modulus is low).

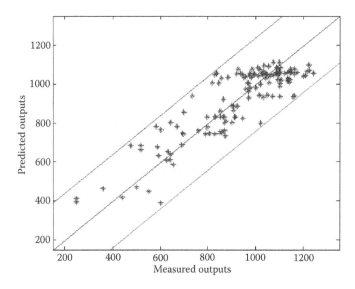

FIGURE 5.8
Scatterplot showing model predicted versus measured yield strength values. (Reprinted from *Journal of Mechanical Behavior of Biomedical Materials*, 53, Datta, S., Mahfouf, M., Zhang, Q., Chattopadhyay, P. P., and Sultana, N. 2016. Imprecise knowledge based design and development of titanium alloys for prosthetic applications, pp. 350–65. Copyright 2016, with permission from Elsevier.)

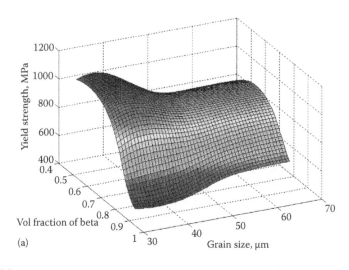

(a)

FIGURE 5.9
Response surface views describing the effects of (a) volume fraction of β and grain size.
(Continued)

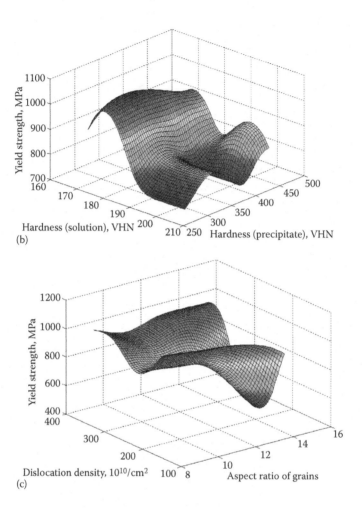

FIGURE 5.9 (CONTINUED)
Response surface views describing the effects of (b) solution and precipitation hardening and (c) dislocation density and aspect ratio of grains on yield strength. (Reprinted from *Journal of Mechanical Behavior of Biomedical Materials*, 53, Datta, S., Mahfouf, M., Zhang, Q., Chattopadhyay, P. P., and Sultana, N. 2016. Imprecise knowledge based design and development of titanium alloys for prosthetic applications, pp. 350–65. Copyright 2016, with permission from Elsevier.)

In this case the number of rules required was 15 and also it is noticed from the rules that the microstructural features have a highly complicated relation with the output. The model predictions are shown in Figure 5.10. The response surface views in Figure 5.11 show that the grain size, the solid solution hardening and dislocation density do not influence the modulus significantly. The elastic modulus initially increases with an increase in β content, but decreases sharply with a further increase, which seems to be the most significant issue in this study. This reveals that the two-phase structure has a higher elastic modulus.

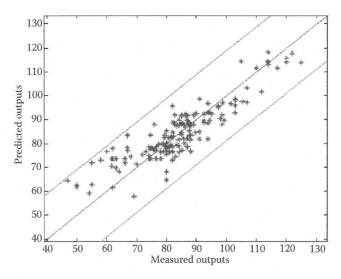

FIGURE 5.10
Scatterplot showing model predicted versus measured elastic modulus values. (Reprinted from *Journal of Mechanical Behavior of Biomedical Materials*, 53, Datta, S., Mahfouf, M., Zhang, Q., Chattopadhyay, P. P., and Sultana, N. 2016. Imprecise knowledge based design and development of titanium alloys for prosthetic applications, pp. 350–65. Copyright 2016, with permission from Elsevier.)

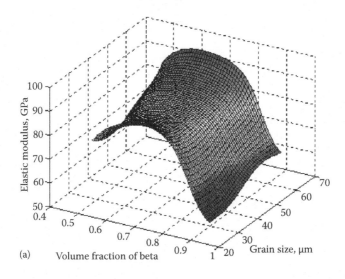

FIGURE 5.11
Response surface views describing the effects of (a) volume fraction of β and grain size, (b) solution and precipitation hardening. *(Continued)*

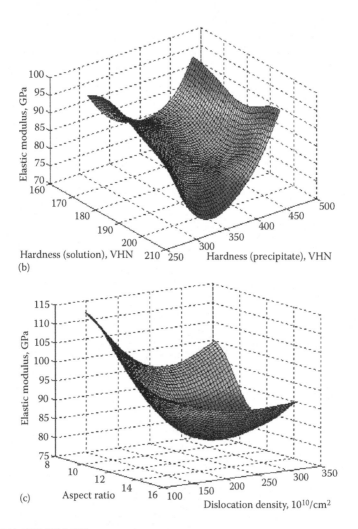

FIGURE 5.11 (CONTINUED)
Response surface views describing the effects of (c) aspect ratio of grains and dislocation density on modulus of elasticity. (Reprinted from *Journal of Mechanical Behavior of Biomedical Materials*, 53, Datta, S., Mahfouf, M., Zhang, Q., Chattopadhyay, P. P., and Sultana, N. 2016. Imprecise knowledge based design and development of titanium alloys for prosthetic applications, pp. 350–65. Copyright 2016, with permission from Elsevier.)

5.3.4 Mechanical Properties of TRIP Steel

Transformation-induced plasticity (TRIP)-aided steels, or simply TRIP steels, exhibit a superior combination of strength and ductility compared to other high-strength steels (Sugimoto et al. 1992). The transformation of retained austenite to martensite during deformation is responsible for its excellent strength–ductility balance, due to continuous work hardening and delayed necking. The complexity of the TRIP phenomenon provides scope for exploration. The chemistry of the steel, that is, the amounts of C, Mn and Si, along with the process parameters, that is, percentage of cold deformation, intercritical annealing time and temperature and bainitic transformation time and temperature, influence the microstructure of the steel, which consists of ferrite, bainite and some amount of austenite and martensite. The outputs considered were tensile strength and % elongation. The volume fraction and distribution of the phases determine the mechanical properties of the steel. In this work an attempt has been made to analyse the experimentally developed TRIP steel data published by researchers during the past few decades using RST. After searching a consistent set of cuts in different methods, finally four reducts or significant variables could be identified: Si content of the steel, intercritical annealing temperature, bainitic transformation temperature and bainitic transformation time. This does not seem to be illogical, as among the compositional variables, Si has the most significant role in creating carbide-free bainite, which increases the carbon content of the austenite and retains it at room temperature. Intercritical annealing temperature controls the initial amount of austenite in the steel before the bainite starts forming, and the bainite transformation temperature and time control the amount of bainite formed. This clearly indicates that the property of TRIP steel is governed chiefly by the presence of bainite and transformable retained austenite. The final reducts are used to generate a set of if–then rules, to capture a general pattern in the available data and to extract useful knowledge regarding the TRIP phenomena. To arrive at a small number of rules that represent the most general patterns in the data, two qualifying values are set for the accuracy and coverage of each rule, respectively 80% and 15%. Rules qualifying both of these values were primarily selected. The following rules relate the tensile strength of TRIP steel to the minimal set of four attributes (Dey at al. 2009):

1. If (Si is moderately high) and (intercritical annealing time is low) and (bainitic transformation temperature is moderately low) then (tensile strength is low).

2. If (Si is quite high) and (bainitic transformation temperature is moderately high) then (tensile strength is medium).

3. If (Si is quite high) and (bainitic transformation time is low) then (tensile strength is medium).

4. If (Si is quite high) and (bainitic transformation time is moderately low) then (tensile strength is medium).

5. If (Si is quite high) and (bainitic transformation time is moderately high) then (tensile strength is medium).

6. If (Si is very low) and (bainitic transformation time is moderately high) then (tensile strength is high).

7. If (Si is low) and (bainitic transformation time is moderately high) then (tensile strength is high).

The rules describing the ductility of TRIP steel are as follows (Dey et al. 2009):

1. If (Si is very low) and (bainitic transformation time is moderately high) then (% elongation is low).

2. If (Si is low) and (bainitic transformation time is moderately high) then (% elongation is low).

3. If (intercritical annealing time is moderately high) and (bainitic transformation time is moderately high) then (% elongation is low).

4. If (intercritical annealing time is moderately high) and (bainitic transformation temperature is moderately low) then (% elongation is low).

5. If (Si is quite high) and (bainitic transformation temperature is moderately low) and (bainitic transformation time is moderately high) then (% elongation is medium).

6. If (Si is quite high) and (bainitic transformation time is moderately low) then (% elongation is high).

7. If (Si is quite high) and (intercritical annealing time is high) and (bainitic transformation temperature is moderately high) then (% elongation is high).

8. If (intercritical annealing time is low) and (bainitic transformation time is moderately low) then (% elongation is high).

The aforementioned rules extracted purely from the data after finding the most significant variables (reducts) clearly reveal the role of the variables in determining the tensile properties of TRIP steel. It is evident that a lower amount of Si is favoured for a higher steel strength, whereas for higher ductility high Si content is required. TRIP steel with a lower amount of Si may contain carbides in the microstructure, contributing to high strength at the expense of ductility. In the case of bainitic transformation time, a longer time results in a high amount of bainite, which increases the strength level, whereas a shorter time allows a higher amount of retained austenite and higher ductility of the steel. It is well known to materials engineers that steel is one of the most complicated materials systems, and among different types of steel TRIP steel is much more complicated because of its strain-induced transformation of austenite to martensite during deformation. But RST is capable enough to find the essential variables and derive rules from the database, which seems to be sufficiently interpretable.

5.4 Potential Future Applications

The concept of extracting rules from data of materials systems using fuzzy set theory or rough set theory has not gathered momentum. This is probably due to a lack of awareness among materials designers regarding the immense possibilities of these tools in extracting useful knowledge from the experimental data developed by researchers or from industry. The simple linguistic if–then rules correlating composition, processing, structure and properties of complex materials systems provide an overall idea of the material system. The linguistic rules also provide a guideline for designing materials with improved performance. The concepts of data mining and informatics-based design of materials are gaining ground, as discussed in Chapters 3 and 4. Thus the idea of extracting rules from the data will also enjoy the attention of computational materials designers in the near future.

There are still some areas in the materials field, particularly in the area of alloy design, in which knowledge gaps within the system often lead to experimental trials based on intuition or thumb rules. In such cases the concept of rule extraction may also get equal attention with statistical or intelligent data-driven modelling techniques. The additional advantage of the present approach is that the easily cognisable linguistic rules it yields should generate interest in using the tools in fields such as alloy design, viz. steel design for improved properties, Al-alloy design to cross the barrier of alloy designation or group and even other nonferrous alloys for specific applications. Fuzzy logic can also be used in developing models using prior imprecise knowledge of a materials system, which is discussed in Chapter 6.

References

Chiu, S. 1997. Extracting fuzzy rules from data for function approximation and pattern classification. In *Fuzzy Information Engineering: A Guided Tour of Applications*, eds. D. Dubois, H. Prade, and R. Yager, pp. 149–162. New York: John Wiley & Sons.

Datta, S., Mahfouf, M., Zhang, Q., Chattopadhyay, P. P., and Sultana, N. 2016. Imprecise knowledge based design and development of titanium alloys for prosthetic applications. *Journal of Mechanical Behavior of Biomedical Materials* 53: 350–65.

Dey, S., Dey, P., Datta, S., and Sil, J. 2009. Rough set approach to predict the strength and ductility of TRIP steel. *Materials and Manufacturing Processes* 24: 150–54.

Ganesh, M. 2006. *Introduction to Fuzzy Sets and Fuzzy Logic*. New Delhi: PHI Learning.

Hin, T. S. (Ed.) 2004. Engineering Materials for Biomedical Applications. *Biomaterials Engineering and Processing*, Vol. 1. Singapore: World Scientific.

Mamdani, E. H., and Assilian, S. 1975. An experiment in linguistic synthesis with a fuzzy logic controller. *International Journal of Man-Machine Studies* 7: 1–13.

Pawlak, Z. 1982. Rough sets. *International Journal of Computer and Information Sciences* 11: 341–56.

Singh, J., and Gill, S. S. 2009. Fuzzy modelling and simulation of ultrasonic drilling of porcelain ceramic with hollow stainless steel tools. *Materials and Manufacturing Processes* 24: 468–475.

Sugeno, M. 1977. Fuzzy measures and fuzzy integrals: A survey. In *Fuzzy Automata and Decision Processes*, eds. M. M. Gupta, G. N. Saridis, and B. R. Gaines, pp. 89–102. New York: North-Holland.

Sugimoto, K., Kobayashi, M., and Hashimoto, S. 1992. Ductility and strain-induced transformation in a high-strength transformation-induced plasticity-aided dual phase steel. *Metallurgical and Materials Transactions A* 23: 3085–91.

Zadeh, L. A. 1965. Fuzzy sets. *Information and Control* 8: 338–532.

Zhang, Q., and Mahfouf, M. 2008. Mamdani-type fuzzy modelling via hierarchical clustering and multi-objective particle swarm optimisation (FM-HCPSO). *International Journal of Computational Intelligence Research* 4: 314–28.

Zhang, Q., and Mahfouf, M. 2010. A nature-inspired multi-objective optimization strategy based on a new reduced space searching algorithm for the design of alloy steels. *Engineering Applications of Artificial Intelligence* 23: 660–75.

Zhang, Q., Mahfouf, M., Panoutsos, G., Beamish, K., and Norris, I. 2011. Multiple characterisation modelling of friction stir welding using a genetic multi-objective data-driven fuzzy modelling approach. In *IEEE International Conference on Fuzzy Systems*, Taiwan, 2288–95.

6

Handling Imprecise Knowledge through Fuzzy Inference Systems

Knowledge is the acquisition of awareness or familiarity of a subject or skill through experience, by assimilating information. The experience may be theoretical through education, or it may be practical. When we talk about scientific knowledge, we understand it comes from a systematic experimentation or study of any system. Previously gathered knowledge or information may also be utilised to explain any observation or phenomenon, resulting in new knowledge. In the case of materials systems, the behaviour of materials could be explained by the knowledge of fundamental physics and chemistry, and that would lead to knowledge of the particular materials system. But this may not be true for all materials systems. The systems whose response depends on several variables and interaction between the variables makes the system complex enough to be explained completely using the fundamental science. Steel and many alloy systems are examples of such materials. In such cases expressing the systems' knowledge mathematically becomes difficult.

One way to develop mathematical models of such systems is to make the system simpler with certain assumptions. This approach definitely has academic interest, but seldom practical applications. The other way out is to ignore the issue of the science behind the system and choose data-driven modelling using statistical or computational intelligence tools discussed in Chapters 3 through 5, and in the process try to extract new knowledge about the system. But some kind of knowledge of the system may exist which may not be precise enough to be expressed mathematically based on the established scientific theory, but can be expressed in imprecise linguistic form. Let us consider the case of microalloyed steel with addition of Nb and B. The strength of the alloy increases as a result of the addition of Nb and B individually, but increases more than the cumulative effect of the two microalloying elements if they are added together owing to their synergism. This is difficult to express mathematically using the underlying physics, as the presence of many other variables actually determines the quantitative effect of the elements. But the aforementioned phenomenon may be easily expressed in terms of a few linguistic if–then rules. Fuzzy inference systems provide an opportunity to use such imprecise if–then rules to be utilised to develop mathematical models to predict the phenomenon. As there are many materials systems in daily use which have such complexity, the imprecise knowledge of the system developed through experience may be utilised to make models of practical utility. The fuzzy inference system thus developed may be refined using experimental data through a concept similar to training of neural networks, and is called the neuro-fuzzy inference system. In this chapter, the concepts of fuzzy and neuro-fuzzy inference systems are explained. Several case studies of applications of such systems are then presented.

6.1 Fuzzy Inference Systems

Fuzzy inference systems (FISs) may broadly be divided into two types, Mamdani type and a Sugeno type (Ganesh 2006), which were previously mentioned in Chapter 5. The first step for developing an FIS is creating the fuzzy rules. The fuzzy if–then rules are, as previously mentioned, a collection of linguistic statements that describe the inherent knowledge of the system and the relation between the independent and response variables. Fuzzy rules in a Mamdani FIS are expressed in the form

> If (input A is membership function a) and/or (input B is membership function b) and/or … then (output P is output membership function p).

For example,

> If (carbon is high) and (manganese is high) then (strength of the steel is high).

There would have to be membership functions that define the fuzzy sets, for example, high, low and so forth. The values of the attribute 'temperature' may have membership in different fuzzy sets simultaneously with varying membership values assigned to each set depending on the membership functions. All crisp values are thus converted to a set of values corresponding to membership values in different fuzzy sets, such as high temperature (input A), high humidity (input B) and a hot room (output P), and similarly for other situations such as low temperature, low humidity and so forth. This processing of an input through membership functions is called fuzzification. The purpose of fuzzification is to map the inputs to values from 0 to 1 using a set of membership functions. Another part in a fuzzy rule is where 'and', 'or' or 'not' exists, which is called the fuzzy combination. The methods of these combinations are called 'T-norms' (Lee 2005) and are described below.

- *Fuzzy 'and'*

  The fuzzy 'and' is written as

$$\mu_{A \cap B} = T(\mu_A(x), \mu_B(x)) \tag{6.1}$$

where μ_A is read as 'the membership in class A', that is, membership of input A in fuzzy set a, and μ_B is read as 'the membership in class B'. There are many ways to compute 'and'. The common methods are one proposed by Zadeh in which the minimum of the two (or more) membership values are taken, that is, $\min(\mu_A(x), \mu_B(x))$, and the other is the product method in which the product of the two membership values is taken, that is, $(\mu_A(x)$ times $\mu_B(x))$.

- *Fuzzy 'or'*

  The fuzzy 'or' is written as

$$\mu_{A \cup B} = T(\mu_A(x), \mu_B(x)) \tag{6.2}$$

Here also two techniques for computing exist. Zadeh proposed a fuzzy 'or' calculation by taking the maximum of the two (or more) membership values, $\max(\mu_A(x), \mu_B(x))$. The product rule uses the difference between the sum of the two (or more) membership values and the product of the membership values, that is, $(\mu_A(x) + \mu_B(x) - \mu_A(x)\mu_B(x))$. Then the consequence part of a fuzzy rule is calculated in the following manner:

1. Calculating the rule strength by combining the fuzzified inputs using the fuzzy combination process, described in the preceding text
2. Clipping the output membership function at the rule strength

    The method is shown in Figure 6.1. The outputs of the fuzzy rules are combined to obtain a single fuzzy output distribution, using the fuzzy 'or'. The fuzzy output thus obtained is converted to a crisp number for the output, through a process known as defuzzification. For defuzzifying the output any one of the following techniques is employed.

    a. Centre of mass: This technique calculates the center of mass of the output distribution to get the crisp number, and can be computed as

$$z = \frac{\sum_{j=1}^{q} Z_j \mu_c(Z_j)}{\sum_{j=1}^{q} \mu_c(Z_j)} \tag{6.3}$$

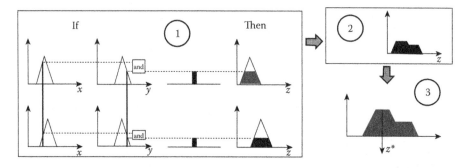

FIGURE 6.1
Fuzzification of inputs, calculation of fuzzy output based on rule strength and defuzzification of output.

where z is the centre of mass and μ_c is the membership in class c at value Z_j.

b. Mean of maximum: This technique calculates the mean of the maxima of the output distribution to find the crisp number, and is computed as

$$z = \sum_{j=1}^{l} \frac{Z_j}{l} \tag{6.4}$$

where z is the mean of the maximum, Z_j is the point at which the membership function is maximum and l is the number of times the output distribution reaches the maximum level. The details can be found elsewhere (Lee 2005).

The Sugeno FIS is quite similar to the Mamdani FIS. The only difference is in the consequence part. Here there is no output membership function; instead the output is calculated in weighted average or weighted summation method, taking the crisp values and fuzzy membership values of the inputs into consideration. The reason to use a Sugeno FIS rather than a Mamdani FIS is that there are algorithms, which can be used to automatically optimise the Sugeno FIS, as in case of adaptive neuro-fuzzy systems.

6.2 Adaptive Neuro-FIS

The adaptive neuro-fuzzy inference system (ANFIS) is basically a process of refining the FIS parameters to improve the predictability (Jang et al. 1997).

The FIS based on if–then rules developed from existing imprecise knowledge can be refined using predicting error optimisation similar to artificial neural networks. The parameters are adjusted to minimise the prediction error using a database. Thus using ANFIS has the following steps:

1. Design a Sugeno FIS with the if–then rules.
2. Develop a database with actual data.
3. Divide the data into training and testing sets.
4. Run the ANFIS algorithm.

ANFIS modelling actually combines the linguistic rule-based modelling method with structural learning abilities, as in neural networks. Here the network's output is expressed as a sum of a number of small neuro-fuzzy systems, each with a limited number of inputs from the main input vector. The output is given by

$$y(x) = \sum_{i=1}^{p} \mu_{Ai}(x) \sum_{j=1}^{q} w_{ji} y_j^c \tag{6.5}$$

where $\mu_{Ai}(x)$ is the ith multivariate fuzzy membership function generated by the fuzzy intersection of the linguistic variables A_i^k, y_j^c is the centre of the jth fuzzy output set and w_{ji} is the weight associated with the corresponding membership function. The steps for training a fuzzy system with the help of a data set using the principle of neural networks include presenting the training data to the FIS and then training the model to refine the model structure. It is to be noted here that the connections and rule bases are kept fixed during training, and only the weights and rule confidences are determined through training. A typical ANFIS structure is shown in Figure 6.2.

The advantage of training the FIS using the principle of neural networks lies with the Sugeno type of FIS, as mentioned earlier. But some limitations lie in this type of FIS, the first and foremost being that the concept of fuzzy sets cannot be applied in the output, and thus defining the whole system in a linguistic manner becomes difficult. Some practitioners may feel that it is easy to describe a system using if–then rules in the structure of the Mamdani type FIS, and it would be better to refine the parameters of the Mamdani FIS to improve the predictability of the model. The best way to approach such a problem is to choose error minimisation using any evolutionary algorithm (Cordón 2011). The method of doing so has been demonstrated and it is finding its use in the materials field also.

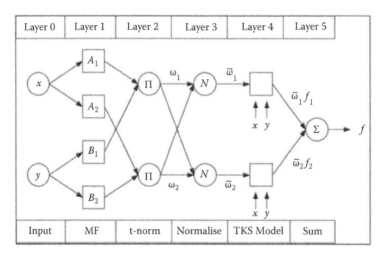

FIGURE 6.2
Two-input ANFIS architecture with two rules. (From Hayer, H., and Nikou, M. R. K. *Petroleum Science and Technology* 32: 1357–64, 2014. With permission.)

6.3 Case Studies

The basic principles of using imprecise knowledge of a materials system in the presence or absence of experimental data were discussed in the preceding text. Some applications of the concept are now discussed in the form of case studies.

6.3.1 Modelling HSLA Steel

The system of thermomechanically control processed (TMCP) high-strength low-alloy (HSLA) steel was previously introduced for artificial neural network modelling in Chapter 4. The system is recalled, as it may help readers to understand the advantages and disadvantages of applying different computational intelligence (CI) tools to the same materials system. It is known that the chemical composition and processing parameters determine the mechanical properties of HSLA steels in a complicated manner. This section attempts to study the effects of those parameters on the mechanical properties of HSLA steels using a Mamdani type fuzzy system (Datta and Banerjee 2005). The composition and the process parameters such as slab reheating temperature (SRT), percentage deformation in different temperature zones (designated as D1, D2 and D3), finish rolling temperature (FRT) and cooling rate (CR) are the input variables, whereas yield strength (YS) is the output. Initially some simple relationships between the inputs and the output are modelled through an FIS, where only a few variables are considered. Finally a complicated model was formulated via an FIS by employing all the input parameters.

Niobium reduces the α grain size, increases the bainite content of the steel and also provides precipitation in the form of carbides or carbonitrides. On the other hand, boron has no appreciable effect when present singularly. Nb and B exhibit a synergistic effect on the steel strength. Ti also strengthens HSLA steel in a manner similar to that of niobium, that is, through formation of carbides or carbonitrides. It also exhibits a synergistic effect with B.

With the help of the preceding knowledge, a three-input FIS is formed, where Nb and Ti are taken within a range of 0 to 0.04 wt% and are divided into two memberships, high and low, as shown in Figure 6.3. Similarly B is taken within the range of 0 to 0.002 wt% with two membership functions. The remaining composition and all of the process parameters of the steel are kept constant. The resultant YS of the steel varied between 800 and 1100 MPa, and was divided into five membership groups, viz. low, low-medium,

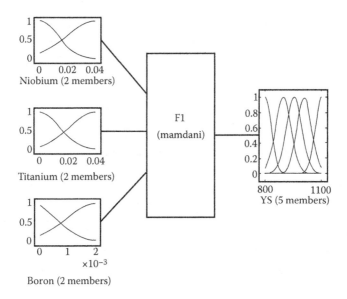

FIGURE 6.3
Membership functions of the inputs and the output variables for FIS. (Reprinted from *Materials and Manufacturing Processes*, 20, Datta, S., and Banerjee, M. K. Fuzzy modeling of strength–composition–process parameters relationships of HSLA steels, pp. 761–76. Copyright 2005, with permission from Taylor & Francis.)

medium-medium, high-medium and high. The nine if–then rules formed to describe the system are given below (Ghosh et al. 2005).

1. If (B is high) then (YS is low-medium) (Nb and Ti are absent).
2. If (Nb is high) then (YS is medium-medium) (B and Ti are absent).
3. If (Ti is high) then (YS is medium-medium) (Nb and B are absent).
4. If (Nb is low) and (Ti is low) then (YS is low-medium) (B is absent).
5. If (Nb is high) and (B is high) then (YS is high-medium) (Ti is absent).
6. If (Ti is high) and (B is high) then (YS is high-medium) (Nb is absent).
7. If (Nb is high) and (Ti is low) and (B is high) then (YS is high-medium).
8. If (Nb is low) and (Ti is high) and (B is high) then (YS is high-medium).
9. If (Nb is high) and (Ti is high) and (B is high) then (YS is high).

The response surfaces show that the model could identify the similarities and differences between the individual roles of Nb, Ti and B (Figure 6.4) from the if–then rules. The predictions by the model are plotted in Figure 6.5.

The manner of strengthening by Cu is different from that of Nb or Ti. It forms a precipitate of ε-copper. It has a synergism with B in this type of steel, as precipitation of Cu is delayed in B-treated steels. But the strengthening effect of Cu is much less than that of Nb. As discussed previously, Nb also has a synergism with B. These three variables are now considered for developing FIS and the relation discussed earlier is again described through a set of if–then rules. The rules are (Datta and Banerjee 2005)

1. If (Nb is high) then (YS is low-medium) (Cu and B is absent).
2. If (Cu is high) then (YS is low-medium) (Nb and B is absent).
3. If (B is high) then (YS is low-medium) (Cu and Nb is absent).
4. If (Nb is high) and (B is high) then (YS is high-medium) (Cu is absent).
5. If (Cu is high) and (B is high) then (YS is high-medium) (Nb is absent).
6. If (Cu is high) and (Nb is low) and (B is high) then (YS is high-medium).
7. If (Cu is low) and (Nb is high) and (B is high) then (YS is high-medium).
8. If (Cu is low) and (Nb is low) and (B is low) then (YS is low).
9. If (Cu is high) and (Nb is high) and (B is high) then (YS is high).

The relation between elemental concentrations and the YS is shown in Figure 6.6. It is to be noted here that the differences in the strengthening capacities of the three elements are more or less revealed in the surface

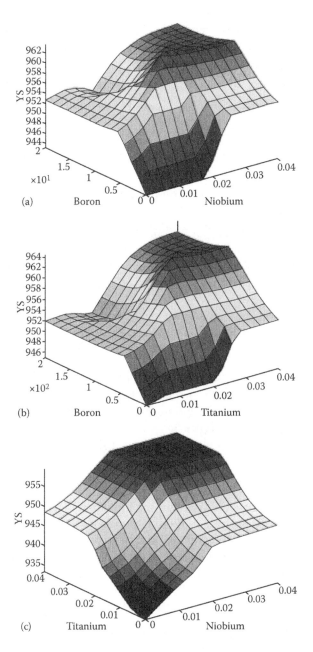

FIGURE 6.4
The response surfaces mapping the relations between (a) Nb–B with yield strength, (b) Ti–B and (c) Nb–Ti with yield strength. (Reprinted from *Materials and Manufacturing Processes*, 20, Datta, S., and Banerjee, M. K. Fuzzy modeling of strength–composition–process parameters relationships of HSLA steels, pp. 761–76. Copyright 2005, with permission from Taylor & Francis.)

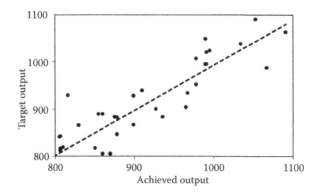

FIGURE 6.5
Actual versus predicted values of yield strength. (Reprinted from *Materials and Manufacturing Processes*, 20, Datta, S., and Banerjee, M. K. Fuzzy modeling of strength–composition–process parameters relationships of HSLA steels, pp. 761–76. Copyright 2005, with permission from Taylor & Francis.)

views, which show the plausibility of expressing the complex imprecise relations between the variables in a steel system in the form of if–then rules and also the capability of FIS to act as a predictive model using such rules only.

Finally, all of the variables are taken together to develop an FIS for predicting YS of thermomechanically processed HSLA steels. Twenty if–then rules are formulated to develop the FIS and the predicted values are compared with the real values of YS (Figure 6.7).

Readers may find certain observations useful for practical purposes. The systems which have fewer variables are found to have better predictability. It is also observed that the performance of FIS depends highly on the formulation of the if–then rules and the manner in which the variables are divided into fuzzy sets. It is difficult to design the FIS when there are large numbers of input variables. The effects of the independent variables on the response variable vary; moreover, some interaction between the variables in the form of synergism as well as antisynergism may exist. Many if–then rules become necessary to define such a complicated system. Though the present exercise could successfully map the input variables to the output space of TMCP steel, there definitely remains scope for further improvement.

6.3.2 Modelling TRIP-Aided Steel

From the experience of the previous work and the problem of handling a large number of variables in developing the rule base, here the system has been divided into several subsystems having a smaller number of variables (Dey et al. 2008). The subsystems are stitched using the system knowledge to develop a complete FIS to describe the complex system of transformation-induced

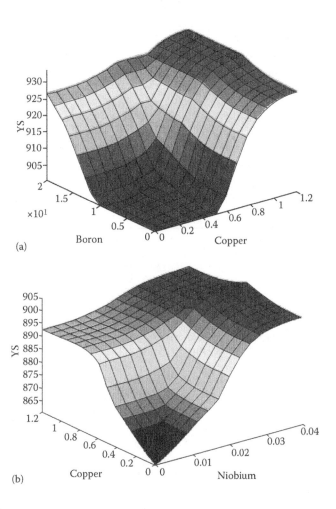

FIGURE 6.6
The response surfaces mapping the relations between (a) Cu–B and (b) Cu–Nb with yield strength. (Reprinted from *Materials and Manufacturing Processes*, 20, Datta, S., and Banerjee, M. K. Fuzzy modeling of strength–composition–process parameters relationships of HSLA steels, pp. 761–76. Copyright 2005, with permission from Taylor & Francis.)

plasticity (TRIP)-aided steel. This system was introduced in Chapter 5, where rough set analysis is employed on it. As previously mentioned, TRIP steel has a composite microstructure of ferrite, bainite, retained austenite and some martensite (Zackay et al. 1967). The transformation of retained austenite to martensite during plastic deformation of TRIP steels results in continuous strain hardening leading to delayed necking, which results in a fine combination of strength and ductility. Other than the composition of the steel, the process parameters, viz. amount of cold deformation, intercritical annealing time and temperature and bainitic transformation time and

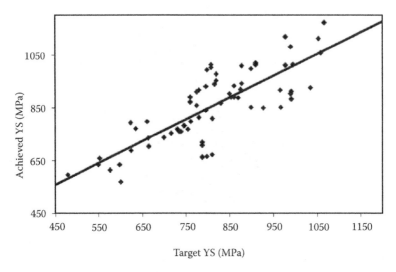

FIGURE 6.7
Actual versus predicted values of yield strength by the FIS having all the variables. (Reprinted from *Materials and Manufacturing Processes*, 20, Datta, S., and Banerjee, M. K. Fuzzy modeling of strength–composition–process parameters relationships of HSLA steels, pp. 761–76. Copyright 2005, with permission from Taylor & Francis.)

temperature are known to influence the microstructure and properties of the product. The lack of precise knowledge about the role of the independent variables on the microstructure and properties of the steel makes it an ideal system to venture into developing an FIS. In this chapter an FIS based on a distributed approach is developed to determine the strength of TRIP steel in the presence of incomplete and imprecise knowledge about the problem domain. The whole mechanism of TRIP steel is expressed from the fundamental physical metallurgy concept through if–then rules. The structure of the FIS is shown in Figure 6.8.

The volume fraction of intercritical austenite depends on the intercritical temperature and the composition of the steel, particularly C and Mn. It is also known that the role of C is more crucial than that of Mn. These factors are represented by if–then rules as follows (Dey et al. 2008):

1. If (the C content is high) and (the Mn content is high) and (the intercritical temperature is high), then (the volume fraction of intercritical austenite is high).

2. If (the C content is low) and (the Mn content is low) and (the intercritical temperature is low), then (the volume fraction of intercritical austenite is low).

3. If (the C content is medium) and (the Mn content is medium) and (the intercritical temperature is medium), then (the volume fraction of intercritical austenite is medium).

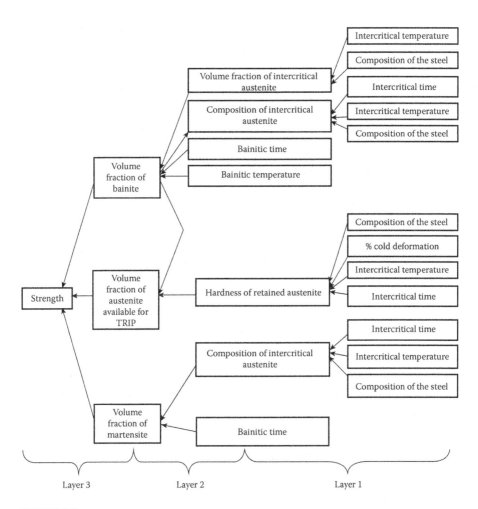

FIGURE 6.8
The FIS developed to represent the TRIP steel system. (Reprinted from *Computational Materials Science*, 43, Dey, S., Datta, S., Chattopadhyay, P. P., and Sil, J. Modeling the properties of TRIP steel using AFIS: A distributed approach, pp. 501–11. Copyright 2008, with permission from Elsevier.)

Similarly the composition of intercritical austenite has another independent variable, intercritical time, in addition to the aforementioned variables. Austenite stabilisers such as C and Mn are highly soluble in the austenite during the intercritical annealing. Therefore, the chemical composition of the austenite during the intercritical annealing is different from the composition of the steel. So the if–then rules are constructed in the following way (Dey et al. 2008):

1. If (the intercritical time is high) and (the intercritical temperature is low) and the (C content is high) and the (Mn content is high) then (the composition of intercritical austenite is high).

2. If (the intercritical time is low) and (the intercritical temperature is high) and (the C content is low) and (the Mn content is low) then (the composition of intercritical austenite is low).

3. If (the intercritical time is high) and (the intercritical temperature is medium) and (the C content is high) and (the Mn content is low) then (the composition of intercritical austenite is medium).

4. If (the intercritical time is high) and (the intercritical temperature is medium) and the (C content is low) and (the Mn content is medium) then (the composition of intercritical austenite is low).

5. If (the intercritical time is medium) and (the intercritical temperature is low) and (the C content is medium) and (the Mn content is high) then (the composition of intercritical austenite is medium).

Similarly the hardness of retained austenite is also described using if–then rules, where C, Mn, Si content, % cold deformation, intercritical temperature and intercritical time were in the antecedent part. This completes the first layer of FISs, where all the input variables are independent variables, that is, the composition and processing parameters. Now we move on to the second layer of FISs, where the outputs of the first layer of FISs along with some of the independent variables, are used as the inputs (Figure 6.8). The volume fraction of bainite depends on the volume fraction and composition of intercritical austenite, the bainitic holding time and temperature. The bainitic transformation time and temperature are the most prominent. Owing to the 'incomplete reaction phenomenon', part of the austenite will not transform to bainite. It is seen that low and high bainitic temperatures reduce the volume fraction of bainite and a medium bainitic temperature produces a high-volume fraction of bainite. Thus the rules become complicated and are given below (Dey et al. 2008).

1. If (the volume fraction of intercritical austenite is high) and (the composition of intercritical austenite is medium) and (the bainitic time is high) and (the bainitic temperature is medium) then (the volume fraction of bainite is high).

2. If (the volume fraction of intercritical austenite is low) and (the composition of intercritical austenite is high) and (the bainitic time is low) and (the bainitic temperature is low) then (the volume fraction of bainite is low).

3. If (the volume fraction of intercritical austenite is low) and (the composition of intercritical austenite is high) and (the bainitic time is low) and (the bainitic temperature is high) then (the volume fraction of bainite is low).

4. If (the volume fraction of intercritical austenite is medium) and (the composition of intercritical austenite is low) and (the bainitic time is medium) and (the bainitic temperature is low) then (the volume fraction of bainite is medium).

Then the other FISs of this layer are formulated. The volume fraction of retained austenite which will be transformed during deformation or straining depends on the volume fraction of bainite and the stability of retained austenite. The volume fraction of martensite varies with the composition of intercritical austenite and the bainitic holding time. So the rules developed for these two microstructural features are used for developing FISs for the subsystems. Finally the FIS for the strength of TRIP steel, the last FIS, is developed. The strength depends on the volume fraction of bainite, volume fraction of austenite available for TRIP and the volume fraction of martensite. The if–then rules formulated are given below (Dey et al. 2008).

1. If (the volume fraction of bainite is high) and (the volume fraction of austenite available for TRIP is high) and (the volume fraction of martensite is high) then (the strength is high).

2. If (the volume fraction of bainite is low) and (the volume fraction of austenite available for TRIP is low) and (the volume fraction of martensite is low) then (the strength is low).

3. If (the volume fraction of bainite is high) and (the volume fraction of austenite available for TRIP is medium) and (the volume fraction of martensite is low) then (the strength is moderately high).

4. If (the volume fraction of bainite is low) and (the volume fraction of austenite available for TRIP is high) and (the volume fraction of martensite is medium) then (the strength is medium).

5. If (the volume fraction of bainite is medium) and (the volume fraction of austenite available for TRIP is low) and (the volume fraction of martensite is low) then (the strength is moderately low).

6. If (the volume fraction of bainite is high) and (the volume fraction of austenite available for TRIP is high) and (the volume fraction of martensite is medium) then (the strength is moderately high).

The model developed was validated using a database generated from published experimental results. Figure 6.9 shows the comparison of the target ultimate tensile strength and the prediction made by the FIS. The prediction results can be claimed to be satisfactory considering the fact that this prediction is based purely on the if–then rules derived from imprecise knowledge.

6.3.3 Machining of Ti Alloy

The third case study is on the machining of Ti alloys (Ramesh et al. 2008). Ti alloys, as we know, are being used extensively in the aerospace industry because of their specific strength, corrosion and erosion resistance and high temperature applicability. But machining of Ti is difficult and requires specialised cutting tools. WC-Co and poly-crystalline diamond (PCD) are recommended by

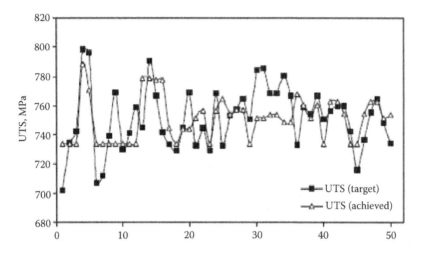

FIGURE 6.9
Prediction made by the TRIP steel FIS. (Reprinted from *Computational Materials Science*, 43, Dey, S., Datta, S., Chattopadhyay, P. P., and Sil, J. Modeling the properties of TRIP steel using AFIS: A distributed approach, pp. 501–11. Copyright 2008, with permission from Elsevier.)

a few researchers as suitable materials. In the present work experiments were conducted primarily on lathe using a PCD cutting tool according to Taguchi's orthogonal array. The cutting parameters used for the experimentation were cutting speed, feed and depth of cut, which were used as input parameters in the FIS. The output responses studied were tool flank wear, surface roughness and specific cutting pressure. As systematic experimentation was conducted, it acted as the guideline for developing the fuzzy rules. The fuzzy rules thus had a basis in the experimental results as well as expert knowledge. Twenty-seven fuzzy rules were developed, and the FIS structure is shown in Figure 6.10.

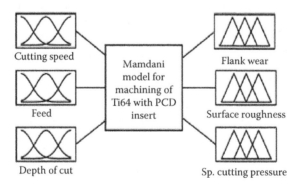

FIGURE 6.10
The FIS for machinability of Ti alloys. (Reprinted from *Materials and Manufacturing Processes*, 23, Ramesh, S., Karunamoorthy, L., and Palanikumar, K. Fuzzy modeling and analysis of machining parameters in machining titanium alloy, pp. 439–47. Copyright 2008, with permission from Taylor & Francis.)

The relationships between the achieved output values and the experimental values are plotted in Figures 6.11 through 6.13. The figures indicate the experimental values and the FIS predicted values are quite close. It can be noted here that data were generated by planned experimentation according to Taguchi's orthogonal array, which is used effectively to formulate the fuzzy rules. Thus the fuzzy rules, though quite high in number, could easily be made to represent the system knowledge in a specific manner. Further, the lower number of inputs also is an important factor for developing effective fuzzy rules. These two factors led to an FIS having extraordinary predictability.

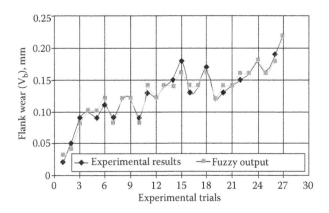

FIGURE 6.11
Prediction of flank wear made by the FIS. (Reprinted from *Materials and Manufacturing Processes*, 23, Ramesh, S., Karunamoorthy, L., and Palanikumar, K. Fuzzy modeling and analysis of machining parameters in machining titanium alloy, pp. 439–47. Copyright 2008, with permission from Taylor & Francis.)

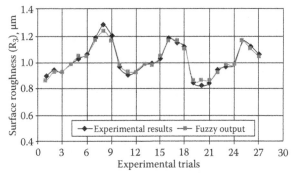

FIGURE 6.12
Prediction of surface roughness made by the FIS. (Reprinted from *Materials and Manufacturing Processes*, 23, Ramesh, S., Karunamoorthy, L., and Palanikumar, K. Fuzzy modeling and analysis of machining parameters in machining titanium alloy, pp. 439–47. Copyright 2008, with permission from Taylor & Francis.)

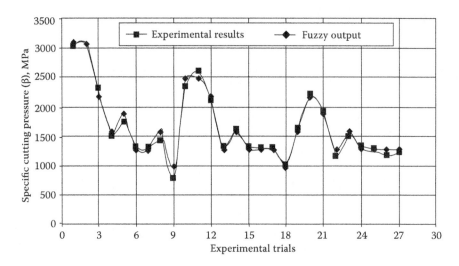

FIGURE 6.13

Prediction of specific cutting pressure made by the FIS. (Reprinted from *Materials and Manufacturing Processes*, 23, Ramesh, S., Karunamoorthy, L., and Palanikumar, K. Fuzzy modeling and analysis of machining parameters in machining titanium alloy, pp. 439–47. Copyright 2008, with permission from Taylor & Francis.)

6.3.4 Ageing of Cu-Bearing Steel

Here a model for predicting the effect of cold deformation and ageing parameters in microalloyed Cu bearing steel is developed using a neuro-fuzzy technique (Ghosh et al. 2005). In this case the rules were initially developed from imprecise system knowledge, and then the FIS developed from the rules was modified using experimental data. The experimental data of the alloy with nominal composition 0.04 wt% C – 1.69 wt% Mn – 0.57 wt% Si – 1.64 wt% Cu – 0.03 wt% Ti – 0.001 wt% B was used. In the first case the relation between input variables, that is, cold deformation, ageing temperature and ageing time with hardness value was considered to develop the model. The critical part of formulating the rules was explaining the issue of overageing at higher time and temperature. The rules were (Ghosh et al. 2005)

1. If (cold-working is low) then (hardness is very-low).
2. If (cold-working is high) then (hardness is medium).
3. If (cold-working is low) and (ageing-temperature is low) and (ageing-time is low) then (hardness is low).
4. If (cold-working is low) and (ageing-temperature is high) and (ageing-time is medium) then (hardness is low-medium).
5. If (cold-working is high) and (ageing-temperature is medium) and (ageing-time is low) then (hardness is very-high).

6. If (cold-working is high) and (ageing-temperature is medium) and (ageing-time is medium) then (hardness is high).

7. If (ageing-temperature is high) and (ageing-time is medium) then (hardness is high-medium).

The structure of the fuzzy inference system developed using the rules is shown in Figure 6.14. The prediction made by the FIS model has an error of 18.3 Vicker's Hardness Number (VHN); after training as an adaptive neuro-fuzzy inference system, it is 12.3 VHN. The simulation plots to describe the role of the variables are shown in Figure 6.15.

When compositional variables are also added with the aforementioned models, things become more complicated. In this case the input variables are the alloying elements (Ti, B and Cu) and the process variables (amount of cold deformation, ageing temperature and ageing time) with hardness of the alloy as the output. The five rules developed to describe the highly nonlinear relations are (Ghosh et al. 2005)

1. If (Ti is not added) and (B is not added) and (Cu is not added) and (cooling rate is low) and (cold deformation is low) and (ageing temperature is low) and (ageing time is low) then (hardness is low).

2. If (Ti is added) and (B is added) and (Cu is added) and (cooling rate is low) and (cold deformation is low) and (ageing temperature is low) and (ageing time is low) then (hardness is low-medium).

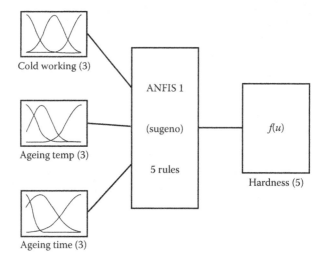

FIGURE 6.14
Structure of the ANFIS with five rules. (Reprinted from *ISIJ International*, 45, Ghosh, S. K., Ganguly, S., Chattopadhyay, P. P., and Datta, S. Modeling the effect of Cu in microalloyed DP steel through neural network and neuro-fuzzy systems, pp. 1345–51. Copyright 2005, with permission from Nihon Tekkō Kyōkai.)

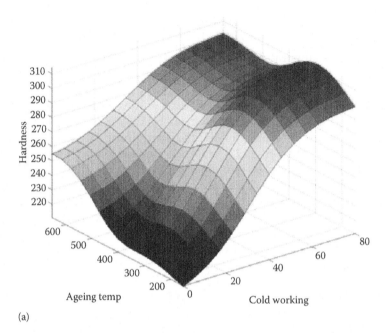

(a)

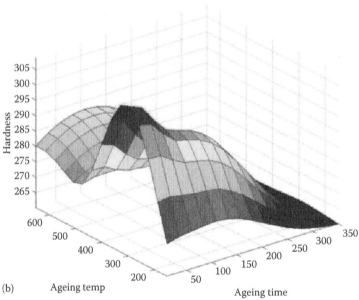

(b)

FIGURE 6.15
Response surfaces for hardness with (a) ageing temperature – cold working and (b) ageing temperature – ageing time. (Reprinted from *ISIJ International*, 45, Ghosh, S. K., Ganguly, S., Chattopadhyay, P. P., and Datta, S. Modeling the effect of Cu in microalloyed DP steel through neural network and neuro-fuzzy systems, pp. 1345–51. Copyright 2005, with permission from Nihon Tekkō Kyōkai.)

3. If (Ti is added) and (B is added) and (Cu is added) and (cooling rate is high) and (cold deformation is medium) and (ageing temperature is high) and (ageing time is high) then (hardness is medium).

4. If (Ti is added) and (B is added) and (Cu is added) and (cooling rate is high) and (cold deformation is low) and (ageing temperature is medium) and (ageing time is medium) then (hardness is high-medium).

5. If (Ti is added) and (B is added) and (Cu is added) and (cooling rate is high) and (cold deformation is high) and (ageing temperature is low) and (ageing time is low) then (hardness is high).

The error was initially 66.8 VHN, but after training the error of the ANFIS was reduced to 27.0 VHN. Thus the method is found to be effective for cases where both system knowledge and experimental data are present. As expected, the predictability of an ANFIS can be improved by increasing the number of rules.

6.4 Uncertainty and Imprecision in Materials Systems

In this chapter the use of imprecise knowledge of a materials system for modelling was discussed. In all cases the available system knowledge is expressed in the form of if–then rules, which in turn are used to develop a fuzzy inference system. But the aspects of uncertainty and imprecision, which are always present in most of the materials systems having a number of factors influencing the final response of the materials, can also be approached in some hybrid ways by amalgamating the fuzzy logic with deterministic, numerical or scientific materials modelling. Normally in *ab initio* or thermodynamic modelling or numerical analysis such a situation is dealt with in a different way. The uncertainty aspect of the model is ignored or judiciously avoided, and the imprecise part is solved using certain assumptions. Most of the time how the uncertainty part could be avoided or how the imprecision could be replaced by a deterministic concept have even become topics of research. But such situations could be handled in a different way by taking imprecision and uncertainty into consideration using fuzzy logic. There may be two approaches for handling such problems; one is handling the uncertainty by making the variable fuzzy and describing it in a nondeterministic method, and the other way is incorporating fuzzy if–then rules as a part of the model, so that the imprecise knowledge could be used without any unnecessary assumptions. These types of applications are gaining ground in different spheres of materials modelling. For example, during modelling of the stress distribution at a microscopic scale using any numerical method such as finite element analysis, handling the grain boundaries is a problem because of presence of uncertainty in the behaviour of the grain boundary. This issue can be approached in a deterministic way, where the grain boundary behaviour can be compared with something known, for example a spring, and the system modelled in that way. Another approach is to describe the grain boundary behaviour in a deterministic way and opt for the fuzzy-finite element method. This type of hybridisation of fuzzy logic with other deterministic methods is also gaining ground. Fuzzy-cellular automata and fuzzy-Monte Carlo methods are examples of some other such applications.

References

Chang, F.-J., and Chang, Y.-T. 2006. Adaptive neuro-fuzzy inference system for prediction of water level in reservoir. *Advances in Water Resources* 29: 1–10.

Cordón, O. 2011. A historical review of evolutionary learning methods for Mamdani-type fuzzy rule-based systems: Designing interpretable genetic fuzzy systems. *International Journal of Approximate Reasoning* 52: 894–913.

Datta, S., and Banerjee, M. K. 2005. Fuzzy modeling of strength–composition–process parameters relationships of HSLA steels. *Materials and Manufacturing Processes* 20: 761–76.

Dey, S., Datta, S., Chattopadhyay, P. P., and Sil, J. 2008. Modeling the properties of TRIP steel using AFIS: A distributed approach. *Computational Materials Science* 43: 501–11.

Ganesh, M. 2006. *Introduction to fuzzy sets and fuzzy logic*. New Delhi: PHI Learning.

Ghosh, S. K., Ganguly, S., Chattopadhyay, P. P., and Datta, S. 2005. Modeling the effect of Cu on hardness of microalloyed DP steel through neural network and neuro-fuzzy systems. *ISIJ International* 45: 1345–51.

Hayer, H., and Nikou, M. R. K. 2014. Multi-component catalyst design for oxidative coupling of methane using ANFIS and ANN. *Petroleum Science and Technology* 32: 1357–64.

Jang, J.-S. R., Sun, C.-T., and Mizutani, E. 1997. *Neuro-Fuzzy and Soft Computing: A Computational Approach to Learning and Machine Intelligence*. Englewood Cliffs, NJ: Prentice-Hall.

Lee, K. H. 2005. *First Course on Fuzzy Theory and Applications*. Berlin and Heidelberg: Springer-Verlag.

Ramesh, S., Karunamoorthy, L., and Palanikumar, K. 2008. Fuzzy modeling and analysis of machining parameters in machining titanium alloy. *Materials and Manufacturing Processes* 23: 439–47.

Zackay, V. F., Parker, E. R., Fahr, D., and Busch, R. 1967. The enhancement of ductility in high-strength steels. *Transactions of the American Society for Metals* 60: 252–59.

7

Evolutionary Algorithms for Designing Materials

Several modelling techniques were discussed in all chapters. This chapter and Chapter 8 deal with the optimisation facet of materials design. Optimisation approaches in engineering can be divided broadly into two types: conventional or derivative-based optimisation and non-derivative–based or population-based optimisation. The latter types of optimisation tools are recognised for their capacity to handle complex functions easily, for a lower possibility of getting stuck in local optima and also for the ease of handling constraints. Among the derivative-free algorithms, two subgroups are drawing greater attention: evolutionary algorithms, a part of computational intelligence techniques, and swarm algorithms. Among the evolutionary algorithms, the genetic algorithm and differential evolution are described briefly in this chapter, and are elaborated with a few applications in materials design. The other types of algorithms (swarm), which include particle swarm optimisation, ant colony optimisation, artificial bee colony algorithm and so forth, are also being used for materials design. This chapter starts with a discussion of the role of optimisation in materials design, which was introduced in Chapter 1.

7.1 Optimisation for Designing New Materials

All types of engineering design have some targets to achieve. It may be improvement of the quality of an existing product, reducing the cost of the product, improving the production process, making the process environment friendly or even developing or inventing a completely new product. Optimisation plays the most important role in achieving any or all of those aspects. The optimisation can have a single objective, for example, increasing the strength of a material, improving the corrosion resistance and so forth, or multiple conflicting objectives, for example, improving the strength and ductility of a material or simultaneously improving the quality and reducing the cost of a product and so forth. In the case of designing a new product engineers also aim for certain objective(s) (Deb 1995). To find the solution(s) for achieving the objective or close to it, optimisation is the most effective tool. In this perspective optimisation tools are being used extensively in the field of materials design.

If $y = f(X)$, where X represents a set of variables $(x_1, x_2, x_3, \ldots x_n)$, a search for a set of X for which y is optimum (maximum or minimum as per requirement) is called an optimisation problem. Many real-world and theoretical problems can be placed in this framework. The variable X has upper and lower boundaries for all of its members (called constraints in the case of conventional optimisation) and the 'feasible solutions' need to be searched without violating these limits. All possible y generated using the X within the limits comprise the 'search space'. The function f is called an objective function, a loss function or cost function or fitness function and so forth. The feasible solution that gives the optimum y is called the 'optimal solution'. In addition to the boundaries of X, there may exist several other constraints in the form of $g(X) = p$ (equality constraints) or $h(X) \geq q$ (inequality constraints), which need to be satisfied simultaneously during the process of searching the optimal solution. This type of optimisation is called constrained optimisation (Rao 1996).

The conventional derivative-based optimisation search from a certain position tries to find the optimal solution by finding the direction. In such cases there always exist possibilities of reaching local optima instead of the global optima (as in case of path 1 or 3 in Figure 7.1a). In such cases the optimisation

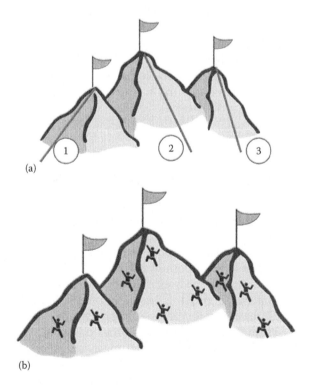

(a)

(b)

FIGURE 7.1
Optimisation (a) derivative-based approach and (b) population-based approach.

procedure needs to be repeated to find the global optimal solution. In the case of an evolutionary algorithm or swarm intelligence the search is population based, in which several feasible solutions are used to try to move towards the best solutions simultaneously, reducing the possibility of getting stuck in local optima (Figure 7.1b). For this reason the genetic algorithm has been so widely accepted in the field of materials design and several review articles have been published on this topic (Chakraborti 2004; Mitra 2008).

7.1.1 Multiobjective Optimisation

Society is always in need of products having conflicting characteristics, such as cars with a high comfort level but lower cost. In the real world, with multiple competing objectives, the concept of the 'optimal solution' changes. It is now not seen as the unique global optimum as in the case of single-objective problems, but a set of solutions providing the best possible compromises among the objectives, known as the Pareto solutions or Pareto front (Deb 2001; Coello Coello et al. 2007). As per the definition of Pareto-optimality, no other solution could exist in the feasible solution space that is at least as good as any other member of the Pareto set, with respect to all of the objectives, and better in terms of at least one. As in the case of Figure 7.2, the bold line shows the Pareto solutions in a multiobjective situation having two conflicting objectives in which both need to be minimised. Here points A and C are two optimal Pareto solutions in the solution space, where A has a higher value for f_1 but a lower value for f_2 and for point C it is vice versa. Both of them are nondominated solutions, whereas point B is a dominated solution. Similarly for max–min, max–max or min–max problems the position of the Pareto front with respect to the feasible solution space will vary. In the case

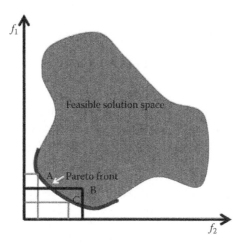

FIGURE 7.2
Pareto front for a min–min optimisation problem.

of designing materials, this concept is being used more and more because the demand for such materials to fulfill the conflicting needs of society is increasing day by day.

7.2 Evolutionary Optimisation Algorithms

As mentioned earlier in this chapter, only two evolutionary optimisation algorithms will be discussed with examples of case studies. The Genetic Algorithm (GA) is a biologically inspired computing technique, which mimics the basic concept of natural selection proposed by Charles Darwin (Goldberg 2002). The algorithm is robust and efficient for most engineering optimisation studies. GA operates on the population of several feasible solutions to produce a solution closer to the targeted solution using the principle of survival of the fittest. At each generation, a new set of solutions is created by the process of selecting individuals according to their level of fitness and breeding them together using operators similar in nature to biological systems. This process leads to the evolution of a population with a better capability to face the environment than its predecessors. In GA a set of feasible solutions is created and the variables in their search space are encoded to form parameter strings, called chromosomes. A single set of parameter strings or chromosomes is treated as a unique identity or a member of a population. Initially a large population of feasible solutions is created with parameter values selected randomly. These solutions are tested using the principle of survival of the fittest, which means the measure of how good that solution is relative to the others in the population, based on the fitness obtained from the evaluation of the objective function. Better solutions survive and have the chance to breed to form the next generation. This selection process is executed by different methods, the most common one being the Roulette wheel method. Breeding takes place through two operators: crossover, which simulates basic biological cross-fertilisation, and mutation, which is essentially introduction of noise. The schematic shown in Figure 7.3 describes the structure of a GA.

The operator for producing new chromosomes is the crossover. As in the case of natural reproduction, crossover produces new individuals so that some of the child's genes are acquired from one individual and some from another individual. This process is executed by cutting two strings at a randomly chosen position and swapping the two tails. A single-point crossover is shown in Figure 7.4. For a multipoint crossover, crossover positions are chosen at random with no duplicates.

Mutation is a random alteration of the genetic information of a member of the population. In actual reproduction, the probability of mutation is rather low, but almost equal for all genes. This principle is maintained here also. The method is shown in Figure 7.5.

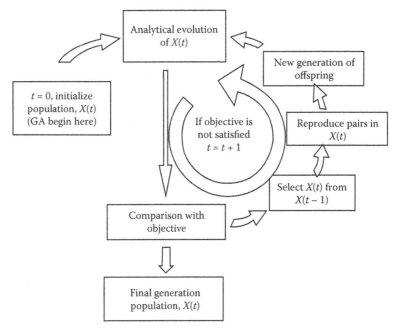

FIGURE 7.3
A schematic representation of a simple GA. (Reprinted from *International Materials Reviews*, 58, Datta, S. and Chattopadhyay, P. P. Soft computing techniques in advancement of structural metals, pp. 475–504. Copyright 2013, with permission from Taylor & Francis.)

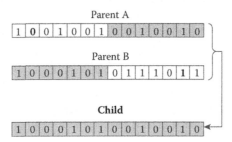

FIGURE 7.4
Single-point crossover.

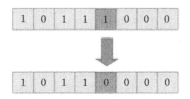

FIGURE 7.5
Mutation effect on an offspring's strings.

After crossover and mutation the fitness of the new generation is measured, and again the individuals with higher fitness are able to breed. The process continues through subsequent generations and the performance of individuals in a population is improved. As the fitness of a population may remain static for a number of generations before a superior individual is found, the application of conventional termination criteria does not hold well. So the common practice is to terminate the GA after a prespecified number of generations and then test the quality of the best members of the population against the problem definition. Such an exercise may be repeated with varied population sizes and generation numbers to ensure that the solutions are not in any local optima. The inherent search method in GA makes it suitable for multiobjective optimisation. The two most important methods of finding the Pareto solution are the nondominated sorting method (Srinivas and Deb 1994) and the niching method (Mahfoud 1995).

The Differential Evolution (DE) algorithm is another population-based algorithm, like GA, similar operators, crossover, mutation and selection (Price et al. 2005). The main difference in the method of searching for better solutions is that GA relies mostly on crossover whereas DE relies on mutation operation. This main operation is executed on the basis of the differences of randomly paired solutions within the population. The algorithm uses the mutation operation itself as a search mechanism and the role of selection operation is to direct the search towards the most potential region in the search space. A nonuniform crossover is implemented in which the parameters can be chosen from one parent more often. The components of the existing population members are used to make trial vectors, where the crossover operator searches for a better solution space. The DE approach has shown better results than a GA and other evolutionary algorithms (Storn and Price 1997) and can be applied easily to a wide variety of complex, multimodal, multidimensional real-valued problems. DE is robust and has been effectively applied in many fields.

7.3 Case Studies of Optimisation-Based Materials Design

Up to this point the case studies were dominated by the development of models towards designing the material directly, through modification of their composition or structure. But materials processing for manufacturing is also an important aspect, as they control the final property of the material. Improving the property, achieving the target composition and structure or producing a defect-free product depends heavily on the manufacturing processes. The cost of the product also depends greatly on it. In this chapter most of the case studies relate to manufacturing processes. The studies are both on Single-Objective Optimisation (SOO) and Multiobjective Optimisation (MOO) using mostly a GA.

7.3.1 Optimisation of Cold Rolling Mills

In this work different factors of cold rolling mills are optimised in an SOO model using a GA by converting multiple objectives into a single objective via weighted summation (Wang et al. 2005). This is a common practice of handling multiple objectives in the case of conventional optimisation, not for evolutionary algorithm–based optimisation. The rolling schedule for a tandem cold strip mill includes the determination of interstand gauges, tensions and rolling speeds at each stand. The aforementioned factors depend on the rolling parameters such as reductions, roll force and torque, rolling speeds and tensions in complex and nonlinear manners. An optimum rolling schedule, which depends on the aforementioned parameters, leads to the desired thickness, surface finish, shape and properties of the rolled plate at a minimum cost. The first step in finding the optimum schedule is developing a rolling model to establish the relationships among the rolling parameters, which would act as the objective or cost function. Then the constraints, such as the mill capacity, need to be defined. The objectives include optimisation of the power distribution, the tension and the optimum flatness condition. Constraints include the roll force and torque limitations, work roll speed references, strip exit thickness, threading conditions and tension limits. In the power distribution part, the objective is to provide uniform power distribution and consistent flatness at each stand. The tension between stands should be kept midway between its lower and upper limits. The lower limit denotes the maximum value of the measured noise under the operating condition, and the upper limit describes the condition for strip skidding and tearing. The third part of the objective is to achieve a perfect shape. For a cold strip, the thinner the strip, the greater is the difficulty in maintaining the proper shape, which depends on the roll force, strip tension, work roll crowns and bending force. Three models developed for the three objectives are combined using a weighted summation principle. W1, W2 and W3 are the three weights, where W1 is the weighting constant for the power distribution cost; W2 is the weighting constant for tension cost and W3 is the weighting constant for the strip shape cost. Users can choose the values of these three constants based on the specific requirements. The results generated by the SOO using GA yield encouraging results. It is seen that the power distribution cost value is reduced by 33.4% when the weight coefficient is assigned a value of 0.4.The same cost is increased from 0.6673 to 0.9714 when the coefficient is lowered from 0.4 to 0.33. A similar variation is observed for other objectives also for varying the weight. This is a typical case of handling a multiobjective problem in a single-objective manner. As mentioned earlier, most real-world demands are multiobjective. But the problem is converted to an SOO problem to make it manageable using the conventional techniques. Derivative-free population-based techniques such as GA have the capacity to handle MOO efficiently and generate the Pareto solutions. In the present case the problem could also have been handled in an MOO mode, and several nondominated solutions could have been generated. In the case that follows studies such as MOO are elaborated.

7.3.2 Gas Injection in Steelmaking

This section deals with the MOO of two conflicting objectives during gas injection in steelmaking process (Kumar et al. 2005). During steelmaking oxygen is injected into the converter or the ladle. Some solid particles are sometimes added to the molten steel along with the gas. Here a simple bottom blown gas-stirred system is considered in which a gas bubble stream rises in a vessel containing molten steel. The vessel has a lining of a high-quality refractory. During gas injection one objective is to achieve a high degree of mixing, which depends on the gas flow rate. But a higher gas flow rate develops high shear stresses on the ladle wall, causing erosion of the refractory lining. An axisymmetric bottom blowing is considered in this study, and to ensure a high degree of mixing in the vessel, the first objective is minimisation of differences in concentration in different parts of the vessel. The second objective is minimisation of shear stress in the refractory wall.

Computation of both objective functions would require complete information on the flow field, which, in turn, is coupled with the temperature field. An acceptable model of turbulence is also very much in order, because in most cases the injection is performed at a fairly high Reynolds number. For an axisymmetric bottom blown system, several assumptions are made, including that (1) the plume is treated as a continuum, (2) the densities of fluid and gas are considered invariant, (3) the fluid is Newtonian and (4) the molten steel is initially at a uniform temperature and so forth. A numerical solution for both the flow and temperature fields is used as the driving model, where the continuity equation, concept of conservation of momentum and energy, the turbulent kinetic energy and its dissipation and mass conservation equation are considered. An equation correlating the plume rising velocity and wall shear stress is used as the other objective function. The MOO on the aforementioned two objectives creates the Pagreto front shown in Figure 7.6. The Pareto solutions provide several solution options with different levels of composition uniformity and wall stress. In such situations the user could easily choose the solution suitable for the particular condition.

7.3.3 Strength and Ductility Optimisation of Low-Carbon Steel

Returning to the issue of materials design directly, this example of application of MOO deals with the conflicting objective of improving strength and ductility simultaneously, in low-carbon ferrite-pearlite steel (Ganguly et al. 2007). In such steels the factors affecting the strength as well as the ductility are solid solution hardening of ferrite, the ferrite grain size, amount of pearlite and the interlamellar spacing of the pearlite. The maximisation of strength along with the ductility is an important area of interest, as it produces steel

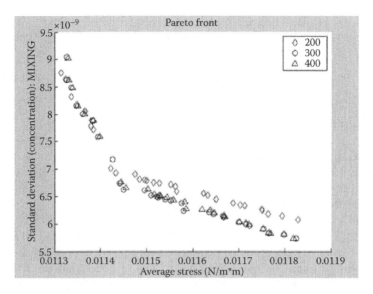

FIGURE 7.6
The Pareto fronts developed in the MOO of the gas injection problem. (Reprinted from *Materials and Manufacturing Processes*, 20, Kumar, A., Sahoo, D., Chakraborty, S. and Chakraborti, N. Gas injection in steelmaking vessels: Coupling a fluid dynamic analysis with a genetic algorithms-based Pareto-optimality, pp. 363–79. Copyright 2005, with permission from Taylor & Francis.)

with better toughness and can be utilised for reduction of weight in the automobile sector and other structural applications. The mechanical properties of steel could be improved through addition of microalloying elements as in case of high-strength low-alloy (HSLA) steel, or through complicated processing as in transformation-induced plasticity (TRIP)-aided steel, both discussed in Chapters 4 through 6. But those approaches increase the cost of the steel. In the present work less expensive and most commonly used steel is considered for property optimisation.

A fully rigorous model for strength and ductility properties in terms of the decision variables from fundamental principles is not available for such complicated systems. Owing to the absence of such model, four empirical models developed through statistical regression analysis, discussed in Chapter 3, are used. The models are for the measurement of flow stress at 0.2% strain, uniform strain, total strain and strain hardening rate (Pickering 1978). Maximisation of these properties is the objective of the present work. The final forms of the regression equations are

$$\sigma_{0.2}\ (MPa) = 15.4(16 + 0.27\ \text{perl} + 2.9\ Mn + 9\ Si + 60\ P$$
$$+ 11\ Sn + 244\ N + 0.97\ d^{-1/2}) \tag{7.1}$$

$$\varepsilon_u = 0.27 - 0.016\ \text{perl} - 0.015\ Mn - 0.040\ Si - 0.043\ Sn - 1.1\ N \tag{7.2}$$

$$d\sigma/d\varepsilon = 385 + 1.39 \text{ perl} + 111 \text{ Si} + 462 \text{ P} + 152 \text{ Sn}$$
$$+ 1369 \text{ N} + (15.4 \, d^{-1/2}) \tag{7.3}$$

$$\varepsilon_{fr} = 1.30 - 0.020 \text{ perl} + 0.3 \text{ Mn} + 0.2 \text{ Si} - 4.4 \text{ P} + 0.29 \text{ Sn}$$
$$+ 0.015 \, d^{-1/2} - 3.4 \text{ S} \tag{7.4}$$

where $\sigma_{0.2}$ is the flow stress at 0.2% logarithmic strain, $d\sigma/d\varepsilon$ is the work hardening rate at 0.2% logarithmic strain and ε_u is the uniform elongation in logarithmic strain, ε_{fr}. The total elongation is expressed in logarithmic strain, perl is the volume fraction of pearlite and d is ferrite grain size in micrometres. All alloy contents are in wt% and N is the free nitrogen content expressed in %. The aforementioned objective functions are subjected to optimisation using multiobjective GA, and the code used in this work is NSGA-II (Deb et al. 2002). The Pareto-optimal solutions are shown in Figure 7.7. Figure 7.8 shows the distribution of variables of the solutions in the Pareto front. It is clearly evident from the figure that, to achieve a good balance of strength and ductility, the favored pearlite content is zero with fine ferrite structure and strengthening of ferrite through addition of Si.

The Pareto solutions developed by simultaneously optimising three objectives can be represented as a three-dimensional Pareto surface, as shown in Figure 7.9. Optimisation through different combinations of conflicting objectives provides different solutions from different aspects of the problem. A user may choose the solution as per the requirement and design the steel composition and microstructure accordingly. For designing new materials the MOO concept is emerging as the handiest tool. The only serious problem in MOO for materials systems is the absence of dependable models to be used as objective functions, which is discussed later.

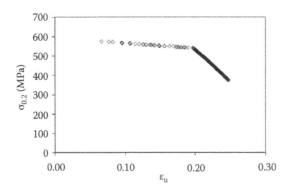

FIGURE 7.7
Pareto-optimal front in optimisation of flow stress at 0.2% strain and uniform strain (true) developed using a GA. (Reprinted from *Materials and Manufacturing Processes*, 22, Ganguly, S., Datta, S. and Chakraborti, N. Genetic algorithms in optimization of strength and ductility of low carbon steels, pp. 650–58. Copyright 2007, with permission from Taylor & Francis.)

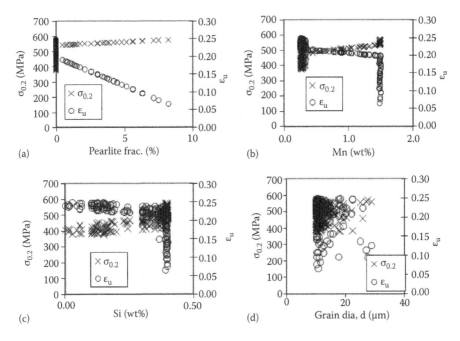

FIGURE 7.8

Roles of (a) pearlite, (b) wt% Mn, (c) wt% Si and (d) grain size (μm) on the optimal flow stress and uniform strain (true). (Reprinted from *Materials and Manufacturing Processes*, 22, Ganguly, S., Datta, S. and Chakraborti, N. Genetic algorithms in optimization of strength and ductility of low carbon steels, pp. 650–58. Copyright 2007, with permission from Taylor & Francis.)

7.3.4 Optimisation of the PET Reactor Using DE

This is an example of MOO using DE (Babu et al. 2007). Polyethylene terephthalate (PET) is one of the important thermoplastic polymers used for manufacturing bottles, fibers, films and so forth. Designing the operation of the wiped PET reactor is essential for PET manufacturing. PET is manufactured using ethylene glycol (EG) and purified terephthalic acid (PTA), where EG is taken in excess and the esterification is carried out in a continuous stirred tank reactor (CSTR) or plug flow reactor (PFR). Antimony trioxide is injected in small concentrations as a catalyst into the oligomer stream leaving this reactor. Then prepolymerisation is carried out to get a 30- to 40-degree of polymerisation. Finally, condensation occurs, where optimisation is important as it controls the final properties of the product. The objective of this study is to eliminate the problems caused by two end groups. The acid end group makes the polymer susceptible to hydrolysis and leads to breakage of the filaments at high humidity conditions during spinning. The vinyl end groups have been shown to be responsible for the unfavorable coloration of PET. Hence the presence of both of these groups needs to be minimised.

Five independent variables are used for optimisation in this study: the reactor pressure P, isothermal temperature T, catalyst concentration (Sb$_2$O$_3$),

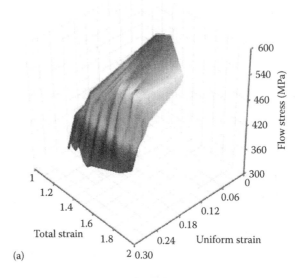

(a)

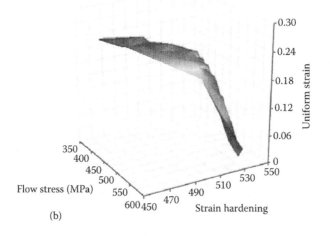

(b)

FIGURE 7.9
Pareto-optimal surface in optimisation of (a) flow stress, uniform strain and fracture strain and (b) flow stress, work hardening rate and uniform strain. (Reprinted from *Materials and Manufacturing Processes*, 22, Ganguly, S., Datta, S. and Chakraborti, N. Genetic algorithms in optimization of strength and ductility of low carbon steels, pp. 650–58. Copyright 2007, with permission from Taylor & Francis.)

residence time of the polymeric reaction mass inside the reactor θ and the speed of the wiped-film agitator N. All of these variables are easily controllable in any wiped-film reactor for PET manufacture. These variables control the concentration of the two groups in question. So the objective functions are designed based on the existing theory of PET reactors. The scheme of

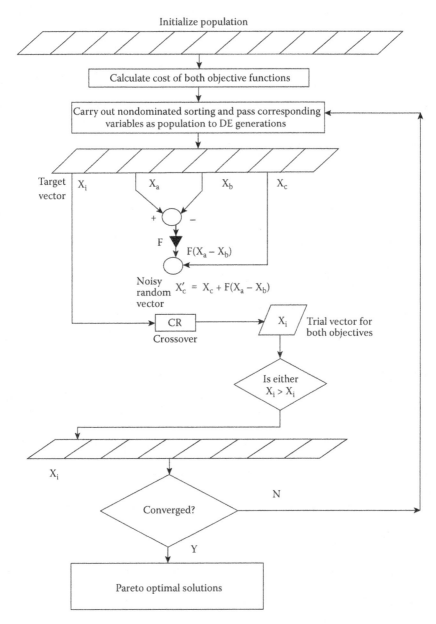

FIGURE 7.10
Schematic of multiobjective DE. (Reprinted from *Materials and Manufacturing Processes*, 22, Babu, B. V., Mubeen, J. H. S. and Chakole, P. G. Simulation and optimization of wiped-film poly-ethyleneterephthalate (PET) reactor using multiobjective differential evolution (MODE), pp. 541–52. Copyright 2007, with permission from Taylor & Francis.)

multiobjective DE, which is used for the optimisation, is shown in Figure 7.10. The variables are allowed to vary in different ways in different separate optimisation exercises and different results are generated from the Pareto front. The Pareto solutions are used as a guideline to the study the behavior of the variables for achieving different tradeoffs between the objectives. The trends of the variables shown in the Pareto solutions are the same for different optimisation search spaces. The trend could also be explained qualitatively from the materials engineering aspect. The results also hint at the possibility of further improvement of the objectives.

7.4 Issues in the Optimisation Approach

Application of the optimisation approach in the field of materials and process design using population-based search techniques is found to be efficient enough for the purpose for which it is used. Evolutionary algorithms make the objective functions and the constraints quite easy to handle. But there are certain issues in the optimisation approach which need to be handled carefully. The first is that of objective functions. The optimisation results are as good as the objective functions. The models used as objective functions for the optimisation process should be adequate to make the optimisation result acceptable. In the case of materials systems, models correlating the independent variables with the performance of the materials are difficult to find for practical uses. Mathematical models based on the fundamental scientific principles of the materials system have a significant number of assumptions and are limited only within narrow boundary conditions. This makes the optimum solutions removed from the actual condition. Thus users should be conscious of the objective functions to use for optimisation. Good data-driven models such as artificial neural networks or fuzzy models can be used, but they have their own issues, which are discussed in Chapter 8. Another issue is that of constraints. Formulating the constraints in an optimisation process is of utmost importance. The reliability of the optimal solutions depends heavily on the fact that the solutions are drawn from the feasible space without violating the system limitations. Sufficient knowledge about the system is therefore necessary. Sometimes executing the optimisation process in a trial manner and analysing the optimal solutions reveals the constraints to be imposed. This indicates that results in the form of optimal solutions should not be considered sacrosanct without sufficient introspection. In Chapter 8 the use of GA in tandem with other computational intelligence tools is explored and these issues are dealt with further.

References

Babu, B. V., Mubeen, J. H. S. and Chakole, P. G. 2007. Simulation and optimization of wiped-film poly-ethyleneterephthalate (PET) reactor using multiobjective differential evolution (MODE). *Materials and Manufacturing Processes* 22: 541–52.

Chakraborti, N. 2004. Genetic algorithms in materials design and processing. *International Materials Reviews* 49: 246–60.

Coello Coello, C. A., Lamont, G. B. and Veldhuizen, D. A. V. 2007. *Evolutionary Algorithms for Solving Multi-Objective Problems*. New York: Springer Science+Business Media.

Datta, S. and Chattopadhyay, P. P. 2013. Soft computing techniques in advancement of structural metals. *International Materials Reviews* 58: 475–504.

Deb, K. 1995. *Optimization for Engineering Design: Algorithms and Examples*. New Delhi: Prentice-Hall of India.

Deb, K. 2001. *Multiobjective Optimization Using Evolutionary Algorithms*. Chichester, UK: John Wiley & Sons.

Deb, K., Pratap, A., Agarwal, S. and Meyarivan, T. 2002. A fast and elitist multiobjective genetic algorithm: NSGA-II. *IEEE Transactions on Evolutionary Computation* 6: 182–97.

Ganguly, S., Datta, S. and Chakraborti, N. 2007. Genetic algorithms in optimization of strength and ductility of low carbon steels. *Materials and Manufacturing Processes* 22: 650–58.

Goldberg, D. E. 2002. *Genetic Algorithms in Search, Optimization and Machine Learning*. New Delhi: Pearson Education.

Kumar, A., Sahoo, D., Chakraborty, S. and Chakraborti, N. 2005. Gas injection in steel-making vessels: Coupling a fluid dynamic analysis with a genetic algorithms-based Pareto-optimality. *Materials and Manufacturing Processes* 20: 363–79.

Mahfoud, S. W. 1995. *Niching Methods for Genetic Algorithms*. PhD diss., University of Illinois.

Mitra, K. 2008. Genetic algorithms in polymeric material production, design, processing and other applications. *International Materials Reviews* 53: 275–97.

Pickering, F. B. 1978. *Physical Metallurgy and the Design of Steels*. London: Applied Science Publishers.

Price, K., Storn, R. M. and Lampinen, J. A. 2005. *Differential Evolution: A Practical Approach to Global Optimization*. New York: Springer Science+Business Media.

Rao, S. S. 1996. *Engineering Optimization: Theory and Practice*. New York: John Wiley & Sons.

Srinivas, N. and Deb, K. 1994. Multiobjective optimization using nondominated sorting in genetic algorithms. *Journal of Evolutionary Computation* 2: 221–48.

Storn, R. and Price, K. 1997. Differential evolution – A simple and efficient heuristic for global optimization over continuous spaces. *Journal of Global Optimization* 11: 341–59.

Wang, D. D., Tieu, A. K. and D'Alessio, G. 2005. Computational intelligence-based process optimization for tandem cold rolling. *Materials and Manufacturing Processes* 20: 479–96.

8

Using Computational Intelligence Techniques in Tandem

The issues of modeling, simulation and optimisation for materials systems using different computational intelligence (CI) tools were discussed in Chapters 4 through 6. In Chapter 7 the issue of optimisation was dealt with using evolutionary algorithm tools. It was also emphasised that optimisation tools play a pivotal role in materials design, as they provide the solutions, in the form of composition or processing routes, to achieve the targeted performance of the materials. The prerequisite for using any optimisation tool for design purposes is one or more dependable objective function(s) mapping the input–output space of the materials system, which is nothing but good predictive model(s). As discussed in Chapters 1 and 2, for complex materials systems good models, developed following the fundamental science principles of the system, are sparse. The available models are, in many cases, not sufficiently capable of mapping the independent variables of the system to its final performance, which is most essential for a successful design of materials. Sometimes the system is assumed to be simple for the sake of modelling it, which does not have much practical use. In such cases data-driven models or imprecise knowledge–driven models using CI techniques can be utilised for modelling and subsequently as objective functions for optimisation. Thus artificial neural network (ANN) or fuzzy models could be utilised as objective functions for optimisation using evolutionary algorithms or other CI-based optimisation techniques. In this chapter such applications of more than one CI tool in tandem are discussed. Examples are provided of ANN models and fuzzy inference systems (FISs) as objective functions and the Genetic Algorithm (GA) as an optimisation tool in both single-objective and multiobjective modes.

8.1 Designing Materials with ANN Models as the Objective Function

In this section designing materials will be approached using genetic optimisation with neural network models used as the objective functions, even as the constraints. Initially steel design through single-objective optimisation is described, and then designing age-hardenable aluminium alloys in a multi-objective optimisation fashion is considered.

8.1.1 Designing Steel with Custom-Made Properties

This section deals with the high-strength low-alloy (HSLA) steel system, which was described in Chapters 4 and 6. The mechanical properties are the important aspects of this kind of steel. Among these, yield strength (YS), ultimate tensile strength (UTS) and percentage elongation (% El) are the most important, as they describe the strength and ductility of the steel. The strength of the steel could be increased through different strengthening mechanisms, but generally these mechanisms have a detrimental effect on the ductility of the steel. But designing steel with high strength with adequately high ductility is considered to be a high-priority target in the field of steel research, as such steel can have a wide range of applications and could be used effectively for priority sectors such as automobiles. This is basically a multiobjective optimisation problem, with two or three conflicting objectives, that is, maximisation of strength as well as maximisation of ductility. One such work was reported in Chapter 7. Sometimes the requirements are different. For a specific application a user may need a specific strength and ductility level, within a range of course. Normal optimisation cannot be applied in such a situation. In this section the mechanical properties of HSLA steel are clubbed into a unitless composite desirability value using the concept of desirability functions (Das et al. 2009). The desirability functions are chosen based on the knowledge of the desirable values of each of the mechanical properties. Optimising the composite desirability is now a single-objective optimisation problem. So primarily ANN models are developed for the two strengths (YS and UTS) and ductility (% El), as no other kind of model exists to describe the properties as a function of the independent variables, that is, the composition of the steel and the thermomechanical processing variables. The outputs of the models are converted to an individual desirability value which is then converted to single-composite desirability. This composite desirability is maximised using a GA. Thus in this work two CI-based techniques, ANN and GA, and a statistical concept are used in tandem to solve a particular type of problem in materials design.

As before, the HSLA steel data consist of the alloy chemistry, the slab reheating temperature (SRT), deformation in three different temperature zones (D1, D2 and D3), finish rolling temperature (FRT) and cooling rate (CR) as the input parameters, and UTS, YS and percentage elongation (% El) as the output variables. Deformation percentages given in three different temperature regions, namely, region of crystallisation, region of nonrecrystallisation and that of a two-phase ($\gamma + \alpha$) region are designated as D1, D2 and D3 respectively. The neural network models, backpropagated multilayer perceptron (MLP), are developed for each of the three mechanical properties. The models have a single hidden layer and the hidden layer nodes vary from 6 to 20, with 16 input nodes and single output node each. The model performance is measured based on training, validation and test error, and the architecture yielding the best predictive capability is used for property optimisation.

Now the predictions of the ANN models are converted to a dimensionless scale (say *d*), called desirability as per the targeted combined property requirements. This desirability function is constructed in such a way that the property values are mapped between 0 and 1 (Harrington 1965). There are several methods through which the actual value can be converted to its desirability value based on the desirability function. The desirability value depends on the shape of the desirability function, as shown in Figure 8.1. As in the figure, the variables are

Y_{LSL}: Lowest specification of *y*

Y_{USL}: Highest specification of *y*

Y_T: Most desirable value (target) of *y*

Y_{LSL-SR}: Lowest specification of *y* for a given target

Y_{USL-SR}: Highest specification of *y* for a given target

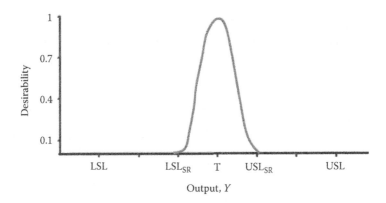

FIGURE 8.1
Functional relationship between physical property and desirability.

Then the desirability function for any variable (*i*th) is defined as

$$
d_i = \begin{cases}
0, \text{ if } X_i < \max(\text{LSL}_{\text{SR}_i}, \text{LSL}_i) \text{ or } X_i > \min(\text{USL}_{\text{SR}_i}, \text{USL}_i) \\[2ex]
\dfrac{f(X_i) - f(\text{LSL}_{\text{SR}_i})}{f(X_{T_i}) - f(\text{LSL}_{\text{SR}_i})}, \text{ if } \max(\text{LSL}_{\text{SR}_i}, \text{LSL}_i) \leq X_i < X_{T_i} \\[2ex]
\dfrac{f(X_i) - f(\text{USL}_{\text{SR}_i})}{f(X_{T_i}) - f(\text{USL}_{\text{SR}_i})}, \text{ if } X_{T_i} < X_i \leq \min(\text{USL}_{\text{SR}_i}, \text{USL}_i) \\[2ex]
1, \text{ if } X_i = X_{T_i}
\end{cases}
\tag{8.1}
$$

where $f(y) = \dfrac{1}{1 + \exp^{-k\left(\frac{y - y_{\text{mid}}}{y_{\text{range}}}\right)}}$; $y_{\text{mid}} = \begin{cases} \dfrac{y_T + y_{\text{LSL}_{\text{SR}}}}{2}, \text{ if } y < y_T \\[2ex] \dfrac{y_T + y_{\text{USL}_{\text{SR}}}}{2}, \text{ if } y > y_T \end{cases}$;

$y_{\text{range}} = \begin{cases} y_T - y_{\text{LSL}_{\text{SR}}}, \text{ if } y < y_T \\[1ex] y_T - y_{\text{USL}_{\text{SR}}}, \text{ if } y > y_T \end{cases}$

A composite desirability scale (say *D*) represents the geometric mean of individual desirability values arising from several properties. Mathematically, it is defined as

$$
D = \sqrt[n]{d_1 . d_2 \ldots d_n}
\tag{8.2}
$$

where $d_1, d_2, \ldots d_n$ are the desirability values for *n* properties of the product. If the product properties have discrimination in their importance on the product quality, then the composite desirability can be modified by using the weighted geometric mean, as suggested by Derringer (1994) and can be written as

$$
D = \sqrt[\Sigma w_i]{d_1^{w_1} . d_2^{w_2} \ldots \ldots d_n^{w_n}}
\tag{8.3}
$$

The use of the method of parallel optimisation can be utilised effectively to improve the product quality in a real-life industrial manufacturing setup, where a specified combination of properties is frequently demanded. To provide equal weight to strength and ductility issues during design, here a simple geometric mean of individual desirability values of UTS, YS and % El is computed to find the composite desirability *D*. The target values of UTS and % El are fixed at 1200 MPa and 40% respectively, whereas for YS, different subranges are constructed in the range of 400 to 1000 MPa at 50-MPa intervals. This is done to explore how the input parameters change with different targeted ratios of YS and UTS. As the targeted extent of strain hardening varies with separate targeted YS, the strengthening mechanism should also vary and that might be reflected in the variables. This may provide an immense amount of information for designing the steel as per requirements.

A GA-based search for optimum solutions of the composite desirability is performed. The maximum desirability values achieved by the optimisation process after 50 generations are shown in Figure 8.2. It shows that there are fluctuations in the desirability values of all the properties at different levels of YS. In some cases the desirability of UTS is low, in some cases YS is low and in some cases ductility is low. For this reason the composite desirability value also fluctuated. The solutions describing the composition and process variables behind the aforementioned best composite desirability for varying target YS are studied. The variables viz. Si (~0.5 wt%), Cr (~0.1 wt%), Ni (~1.8 wt%), Mo (~0.55 wt%), Ti (~0.07 wt%), B (~0.002 wt%), D1 (~47%), D2 (~29%) and SRT (~1050°C) are found to have almost constant values, as shown in the parentheses, for all optimisation conditions. The variations in other input parameters are shown in Figure 8.3. Studying the role of the variables reveals that the solutions are dominated by the elements which give solid solution hardening when the steel has high YS, which means less strain hardening is required. On the other hand, for lower values of YS, precipitate-forming elements such as Nb and Cu predominate.

In this optimisation study all the compositional process variables are allowed to vary freely. But there may be a situation in which the steel composition can be varied, but the process variable needs to remain fixed because of mill constraints. Similarly in certain situations the property combination needs to be achieved on supplied steel (fixed composition) while varying the process variables. The role

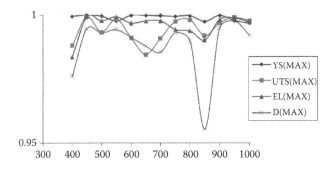

FIGURE 8.2
Composite desirability and desirability for different physical properties. (Reprinted from *Computational Materials Science*, 45, Das, P., Mukherjee, S., Ganguly, S., Bhattacharyay, B. K. and Datta, S. Genetic algorithm based optimization for multi-physical properties of HSLA steel through hybridization of neural network and desirability function, pp. 104–10. Copyright 2009, with permission from Elsevier.)

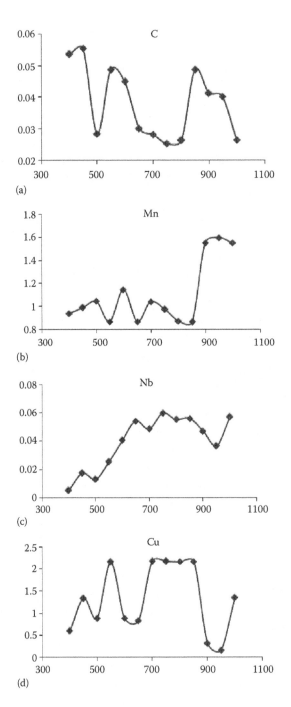

FIGURE 8.3

Variation of suggested alloying additions and process parameters for achieving targeted strength level for (a) carbon, (b) manganese, (c) niobium and (d) copper. *(Continued)*

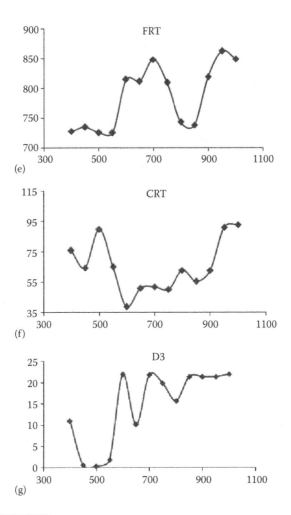

FIGURE 8.3 (CONTINUED)
Variation of suggested alloying additions and process parameters for achieving targeted strength level for (e) finish rolling temperature, (f) cooling rate and (g) deformation in the two phase region. (Reprinted from *Computational Materials Science*, 45, Das, P., Mukherjee, S., Ganguly, S., Bhattacharyay, B. K. and Datta, S. Genetic algorithm based optimization for multiphysical properties of HSLA steel through hybridization of neural network and desirability function, pp. 104–10. Copyright 2009, with permission from Elsevier.)

of the input variables in such situations can also be observed in this way and a deep understanding of designing the steel with any target property combination and in any constrained condition could be gained.

8.1.2 Designing Novel Age-Hardenable Aluminium Alloys

Age-hardenable aluminium alloys, the alloy which is precipitation hardened during heat treatment, are mostly the Al–Cu (2XXX), Al–Mg–Si (6XXX) and

Al–Zn–Mg (7XXX) series of alloys. The second phase is dissolved at a high temperature and then quenched to obtain supersaturated solid solutions, which are aged at a lower temperature to obtain fine precipitates in the matrix. This precipitation hardening process is the most important strengthening mechanism for aluminium alloys (Dey et al. 2016). The precipitations have a detrimental effect on the ductility of the alloy. To improve the strength ductility balance of the alloy judicial addition of alloying elements along with a proper heat treatment schedule is required. This kind of improved performance might be achieved if the boundaries of the series of alloys are crossed and if the effects of the precipitates of the different series could be incorporated. To design such novel age-hardenable Al alloys multiobjective optimisation is implemented using GA, as there are two conflicting objectives in the form of high strength and high ductility. As no accepted physical relation exists that can describe the strength and ductility of Al alloys in terms of the predictor variables, ANN has been used to frame such a relation. Three ANN models for strength (YS or UTS) and ductility (% El) are used as objective functions for the optimisation. The database generated had the chemical composition and the processing parameters as the input variables and the mechanical properties as the output variables for all three series of age-hardenable alloys. These data are used for training the ANN models (Figure 8.4). As the mechanical properties of Al alloys depend heavily on the testing temperature, the data were divided into three groups, the first one for the properties tested at ambient temperature, the second one for the subzero temperature properties, and the third one for the high temperature. Before designing alloys using GA, a sensitivity analysis of the ANN models is performed. An understanding of the relative influence of the alloying elements on the final material properties is important but difficult to identify in the case of ANN models owing to the complex hidden relationships. The sensitivity analysis is one method to get this done, where the hidden-input and hidden-output connection weights are used to calculate the importance of the variables (Olden et al. 2004). Figure 8.5 shows the sensitivity plots generated from the ANN model predicting the room temperature properties. It is seen that almost all of the alloying elements have a profound positive effect on the strength, which is not true in the case of ductility. Similar plots for other variables are also generated, which are not shown in this book.

Certain issues need to be resolved before going into the optimisation process. During optimisation, when the solutions are developed the solution treatment should be constrained. As the solutionising is done within the single-phase region, but below the solidus temperature to avoid melting of the alloy, the temperature should be kept within a narrow range. The ageing temperature is also one which depends heavily on the composition of the alloys. Thus two constraints need to be formulated. Two ANN models, predicting the solutionising temperature (T_{soln}) and ageing temperature (T_{age})

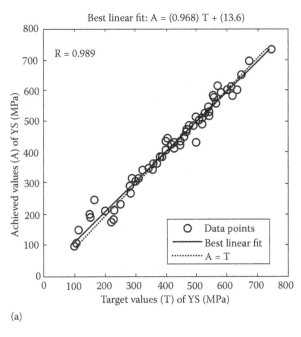

(a)

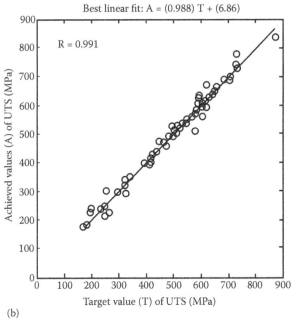

(b)

FIGURE 8.4
Scatterplot for low temperature showing target versus achieved values for (a) YS and (b) UTS
as predicted by ANN models.   (*Continued*)

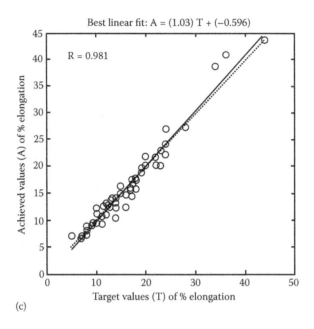

(c)

FIGURE 8.4 (CONTINUED)
Scatterplot for low temperature showing target versus achieved values for (c) % El as predicted by ANN models. (Reprinted from *Materials and Design*, 92, Dey, S., Sultana, N., Kaiser, M. S., Dey, P. and Datta, S. Computational intelligence based design of age-hardenable aluminium alloys for different temperature regimes, pp. 522–34. Copyright 2016, with permission from Elsevier.)

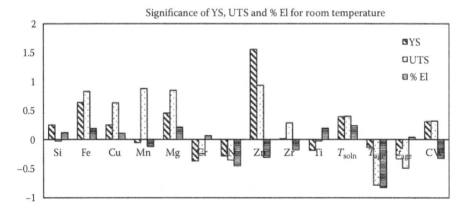

FIGURE 8.5
Sensitivity plots for trained ANN models for YS, UTS and % El using the connection weight method for room temperature. (Reprinted from *Materials and Design*, 92, Dey, S., Sultana, N., Kaiser, M. S., Dey, P. and Datta, S. Computational intelligence based design of age-hardenable aluminium alloys for different temperature regimes, pp. 522–34. Copyright 2016, with permission from Elsevier.)

with composition as the predictors, are developed separately for using them as constraints. The constraints applied during optimisation are as follows:

- The sum of the weight percent of alloying elements is kept at 10 wt% maximum as a constraint, as higher alloy content decreases the toughness of the alloy.
- A tolerance of ±25°C is given to the T_{soln} prediction of the ANN model.
- Similarly, a tolerance of ±25°C is given to the T_{age}.

The multiobjective optimisation for maximisation of strength and ductility using the ANN models as the objective functions, and the previously described constraints using GA, are used to develop the optimised Pareto solutions, as shown in Figure 8.6 for properties at room temperature. It is to be noted here that three objectives are optimised together and in such a situation the non-dominated solutions create a three-dimensional Pareto surface. Figure 8.6 is a two-dimensional projection of that surface. The optimum solutions are analysed further and the variations of the input variables with increasing YS values in the Pareto surface are plotted in Figure 8.7. It is seen that the variation in YS in the optimum solutions is due mainly to variations in Cu, Mn, Mg, Zr and Ti. The other variables remained almost constant. Cu is around 2.0 wt%; Mn is near the upper limit; and Mg, Zr and Ti have low values. Similar exercises of optimisation and analyses of the Pareto solutions are also done for the low-temperature and high-temperature properties of the alloys. This whole exercise now provides a huge range of solutions with different combinations of strength and ductility at different temperature ranges and users have their choice.

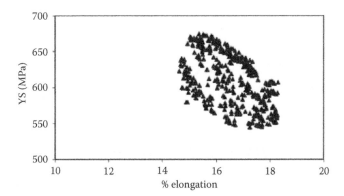

FIGURE 8.6
Pareto front of % El versus YS showing the optimised combination of generation and population size for room temperature developed via multiobjective GA. (Reprinted from *Materials and Design*, 92, Dey, S., Sultana, N., Kaiser, M. S., Dey, P. and Datta, S. Computational intelligence based design of age-hardenable aluminium alloys for different temperature regimes, pp. 522–34. Copyright 2016, with permission from Elsevier.)

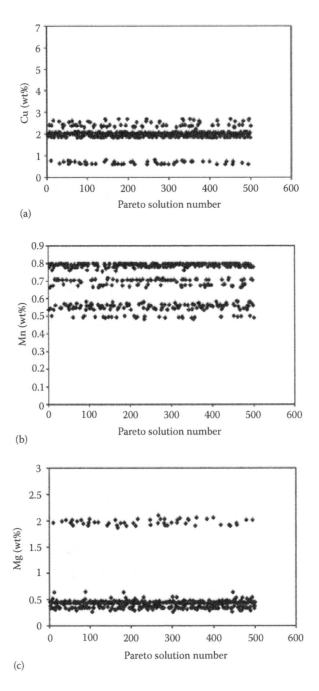

FIGURE 8.7
Variation of (a) Cu, (b) Mn and (c) Mg respectively in Pareto solutions with YS in ascending order in the room temperature regime.   (*Continued*)

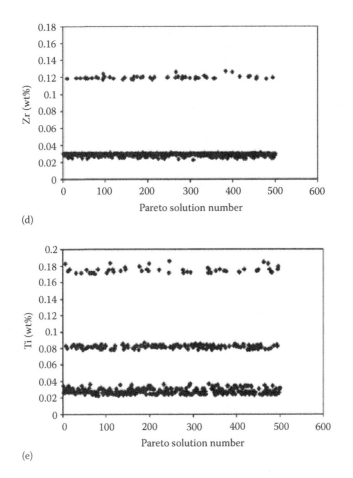

FIGURE 8.7 (CONTINUED)
Variation of (d) Zr and (e) Ti respectively in Pareto solutions with YS in ascending order in the room temperature regime. (Reprinted from *Materials and Design*, 92, Dey, S., Sultana, N., Kaiser, M. S., Dey, P. and Datta, S. Computational intelligence based design of age-hardenable aluminium alloys for different temperature regimes, pp. 522–34. Copyright 2016, with permission from Elsevier.)

8.1.3 Optimum Processing for Better Shape Memory Effect of Nitinol

In the previous example of alloy design the target is to find the composition for developing an Al alloy with better performance. In the present case study the composition Ni–Ti shape memory alloy (SMA) is fixed. GA-based multi-objective optimisation is used for designing the process to obtain the best performance from the alloy (Sinha et al. 2013). It is known that SMAs undergo a reversible phase transformation between the low-temperature martensite and high-temperature austenite phases (Duerig et al. 1990), and in the process can remember its original shape. Ni–Ti alloy, also known as nitinol, is a well-known SMA with enormous possibilities for functional applications. This study aims at optimisation of the process parameters of the Ti-(~49 wt%) Ni alloy for trading off between the mechanical properties and shape recovery behaviour of the alloy using ANN and GA. The database used for developing the ANN model was completely generated by the authors. The processing adopted is basically deformation (rolling) at varied temperature and post-working heat treatment. So it consists of four input variables: deformation temperature, amount of deformation, ageing temperature and ageing time. The output variables are shape recovery ratio, hardness and elastic modulus, respectively. Three separate ANN models are developed which are subsequently used as the objective functions for the multiobjective optimisation of mechanical properties and shape memory behaviour.

The Pareto front developed through multiobjective optimisation of hardness and shape recovery ratio using GA is shown in Figure 8.8. The Pareto solutions are sorted, as in the previous case of Al alloys, in ascending order of the hardness. In this case, a lower solution number depicts a higher shape recovery ratio and a higher solution number depicts high hardness values. Figure 8.9 describes the values of different process parameters in the said order preferred for the optimum combination of hardness and shape recovery ratio. It is seen from Figure 8.9 that low deformation temperature (80–100 K) and a low amount of deformation are preferred for an adequately high shape recovery ratio. It is also observed that ageing is not a preferred processing route to achieve such properties. Thus the optimum solutions clearly indicate that a low amount of deformation at low deformation temperature without any heat treatment can provide the best balance between shape recovery ratio and hardness.

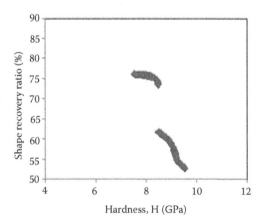

FIGURE 8.8
Pareto-optimal front developed through GA-based multiobjective optimisation of hardness and shape recovery ratio. (Reprinted from *Materials and Design*, 46, Sinha, A., Sikdar (Dey), S., Chattopadhyay, P. P. and Datta, S. Optimization of mechanical property and shape recovery behavior of Ti-(~49 wt%) Ni alloy using artificial neural network and genetic algorithm, pp. 227–34, Copyright 2013. with permission from Elsevier.)

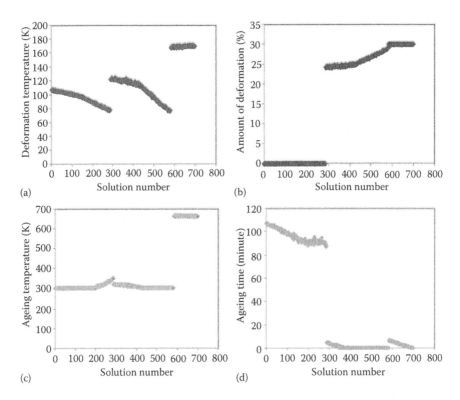

FIGURE 8.9
Variation of (a) deformation temperature, (b) amount of deformation, (c) ageing temperature and (d) ageing time with increasing hardness in the optimum solutions. (Reprinted from *Materials and Design*, 46, Sinha, A., Sikdar (Dey), S., Chattopadhyay, P. P. and Datta, S. Optimization of mechanical property and shape recovery behavior of Ti-(~49 wt%) Ni alloy using artificial neural network and genetic algorithm, pp. 227–34. Copyright 2013, with permission from Elsevier.)

The process is repeated to achieve maximisation of shape recovery ratio and the ratio of hardness to elastic modulus (H/E). As before, the ANN model for the shape recovery ratio is used as one objective function, and the ratio of the predictions of the ANN models for hardness and elastic modulus is used as the objective function of H/E. The four input variables were plotted against ascending H/E ratio as shown in Figure 8.10. The figure shows that a small deformation at around 100 K without any subsequent ageing is preferred for a good combination of H/E and shape recovery ratio.

Thus the multiobjective optimisation of the shape recovery ratio against hardness and H/E ratio has indicated that the most favourable conditions for achieving the best combination of shape recovery ratio and mechanical properties are low deformation temperature, low amount of deformation and low ageing temperature.

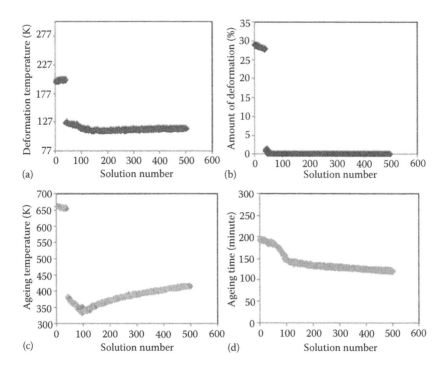

FIGURE 8.10

Variation of (a) deformation temperature, (b) amount of deformation, (c) ageing temperature and (d) ageing time with increasing H/E ratio in the optimum solutions. (Reprinted from *Materials and Design*, 46, Sinha, A., Sikdar (Dey), S., Chattopadhyay, P. P. and Datta, S. Optimization of mechanical property and shape recovery behavior of Ti-(~49 wt%) Ni alloy using artificial neural network and genetic algorithm, pp. 227–34. Copyright 2013, with permission from Elsevier.)

8.2 Polymer Composite Design with Fuzzy Models as the Objective Function

This is another example of an application of multiobjective optimisation for designing polymer composites with higher thermal conductivity and less stiffness (Nandi et al. 2012). But here the objective functions are of different types. An FIS is used for equivalent thermal conductivity of the particle-reinforced polymer composite, where the fuzzy rules are extracted using GA, similar to cases discussed in Chapter 5. The equivalent modulus of elasticity is represented by an existing mechanistic model. The design issue is related to developing better materials for the soft tooling process, where reducing the cooling tome of the wax pattern may significantly increase the productivity. The mould materials used for creating the pattern is silicone rubber or polyurethane because of their flexibility. Addition of particulate fillers in the mould material may enhance its equivalent thermal conductivity but the equivalent modulus of elasticity will be raised, hampering the flexibility. Thus owing to the presence of conflicting objectives, this materials design problem is dealt with as a multiobjective optimisation problem.

In the absence of a proper model for describing the thermal conductivity of the composite, a model of equivalent thermal conductivity (k_c) for particle-reinforced polymer composites, based on a genetic fuzzy system, was developed. The proposed genetic fuzzy model of k_c is based on the Sugeno type fuzzy model, discussed in Chapters 5 and 6, which is also known as the Takagi, Sugeno and Kang (TSK) FIS. As mentioned earlier, in this type of FIS the rules are expressed in the following form:

If x_1 is A_1 and x_2 is A_2 and...... x_4 is A_4, then $y = f(x_1, x_2, x_3, x_4)$,

where $A_1,..., A_4$ are the fuzzy subsets of the input variables, $x_1, ..., x_4$, respectively. The rules are generated from published experimental data. The effectiveness of the model was tested with newly measured thermal conductivities of different polymeric flexible mould composites and it was found to perform better than the existing models. The model also found to be generic and applicable to a wide range of two-phase particle-reinforced polymer composites.

The authors considered the equivalent modulus of elasticity model of particle-reinforced polymer composites proposed by Lielens et al. (1998), where the equivalent modulus of elasticity of polymer composite is

$$E_c = \frac{9K_cG_c}{3K_c + G_c}$$

where E_c (in N/mm²), K_c (in N/mm²) and G_c (in N/mm²) are the equivalent modulus of elasticity, bulk modulus and shear modulus of polymer composite, respectively. The bulk and shear moduli (K_c and G_c) are formulated based on the normalisation of the upper and lower bounds as suggested by Hashim and Shtrikman (1963)

$$K_c = \frac{1}{\dfrac{1-f}{K_{H-S}^L} + \dfrac{f}{K_{H-S}^U}} \quad \text{and} \quad G_c = \frac{1}{\dfrac{1-f}{G_{H-S}^L} + \dfrac{f}{G_{H-S}^U}}$$

where $f = \dfrac{V_f + V_f^2}{2}$ and the upper and lower bounds of equivalent bulk modulus (K_{H-S}^U and K_{H-S}^L, respectively) and shear modulus (G_{H-S}^U and G_{H-S}^L, respectively) of composite materials are also proposed by Hashim and Shtrikman (1963).

Thus for multiobjective optimisation, now we have two objective functions.

$$k_c = f(k_m, k_f, P_s, S_f, T, V_f)$$

$$E_c = f(E_m, K_f, G_f, V_f)$$

where k_c and E_c are the equivalent thermal conductivity (in W/m-k) and modulus of elasticity (in GPa) of particle-reinforced mould materials, respectively. k_m (in W/m-k) and E_m (in GPa) are the thermal conductivity and modulus of elasticity, respectively of mould material (polymer). k_f, P_s, S_f, T and V_f are the thermal conductivity of filler material (in W/m-k), filler particle size (in micron), shape factor of particle, temperature (in °C) and volume fraction of filler. G_f is the shear modulus of filler material, in GPa; K_f is the bulk modulus of filler material, in GPa; and E_f (in GPa) is the modulus of elasticity of filler material.

The most interesting part of this particular case is the constraint formulation. During the optimisation search process the attribute values will evolve, but the values of modulus of elasticity (E_f) and thermal conductivity (k_f) of a particular solution has to be such that a material of such property combination should be available, or at least exist in the nature. For that reason the E_f and k_f of the basic metallic fillers that are commonly available in the market in the form of particles are plotted in Figure 8.11. After analysing the values of E_f and k_f, eight zones (denoted by the numbers 0 to 7) are identified in which most of the metallic filler materials lie. These eight zones represent

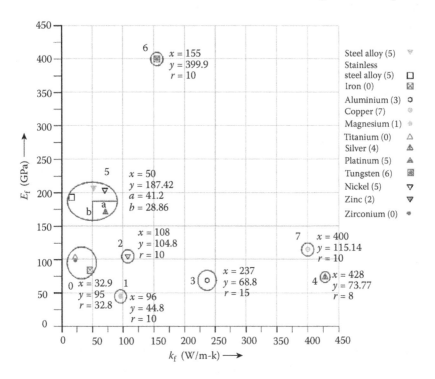

FIGURE 8.11

Plot of E_f versus k_f for various metallic fillers and identification of zones. (Reprinted from *Applied Soft Computing*, 12, Nandi, A. K., Deb, K., Ganguly, S. and Datta, S. Investigating the role of metallic fillers in particulate reinforced flexible mould material composites using evolutionary algorithms, pp. 28–39. Copyright 2012, with permission from Elsevier.)

the constraint for feasible optimum filler material. This means that any solution having E_f and k_f values lying outside of these zones will be treated as an infeasible solution. There is another important constraint, which is the maximum loading level or maximum packing fraction. This limit of adding filler materials is also set as a constraint using a suitable expression.

NSGAII (an elitist nondominated sorting GA) (Deb et al. 2002) and SPEA2 (an improved version of Strength Pareto Evolutionary Algorithm) (Zitzler et al. 2001) are used here for the optimisation. The Pareto fronts obtained using NSGAII are presented for a particulate metallic filler–filled silicone rubber composite system and a polyurethane system in Figure 8.12. It is seen

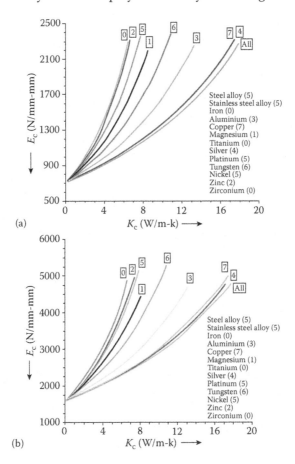

FIGURE 8.12
Pareto-optimal fronts for optimisation of K_c and E_c developed using NSGAII, considering the feasible zones as constraints, for (a) silicone rubber composite system and (b) polyurethane composite system with metallic filler. (Reprinted from *Applied Soft Computing*, 12, Nandi, A. K., Deb, K., Ganguly, S. and Datta, S. Investigating the role of metallic fillers in particulate reinforced flexible mould material composites using evolutionary algorithms, pp. 28–39. Copyright 2012, with permission from Elsevier.)

that if the performance of the individual metal particles is considered, the best performing materials are silver, copper, aluminium and tungsten, in the order mentioned. This is expected, as these metals have the highest thermal conductivity and also do not have a much higher elastic modulus. But if the cost factor, which is also important for materials design, is incorporated then definitely the aluminium filler will be the best choice, as it is quite less expensive than the others.

8.3 Other Possible Approaches

In this chapter all of the case studies on applications of more than one CI technique in tandem ended with optimisation using GA. This is quite relevant, as optimisation is really important for designing materials. It can be single-objective optimisation or multiobjective optimisation as per the requirement of the problem. The optimisation can also be done using other evolutionary or swarm algorithms. In my experience, one algorithm may be marginally better than the other in a particular case and marginally worse in another. Whichever algorithm is used, the target is ultimately to develop good feasible solutions for developing new improved materials.

Besides this particular sequence of modelling and optimisation, there may be other situations where the two methods may be hybridised or used together. In Chapter 5, the method of fuzzy rule extraction was discussed, where GA or other optimisation tools are being used extensively. Similarly, reduct calculation and rule formation using Rough Set Theory are also being fine tuned using GA to achieve the optimum result. Modification of an FIS using the principle of neural network, better known as adaptive neuro-FIS, is another quite common application. ANN is being trained using GA, without going into any derivative-based error minimisation algorithm. This training is also done for use in multiobjective optimisation, if something additional needs to be incorporated in the weights and biases other than searching the minimum error only.

All of these possibilities can be used for materials design to tackle the complexity or peculiarity of the problem. The researcher needs to define the problem first in a specific manner. Then the methodology to be adopted can be formulated. But, for that, one has to have an idea about the usages of the CI tools and the opportunities to use them in combination. In this chapter effort is made to provide some glimpses of such applications.

References

Das, P., Mukherjee, S., Ganguly, S., Bhattacharyay, B. K. and Datta, S. 2009. Genetic algorithm based optimization for multi-physical properties of HSLA steel through hybridization of neural network and desirability function. *Computational Materials Science* 45: 104–10.

Deb, K., Pratap, A., Agarwal, S. and Meyarivan, T. 2002. A fast and elitist multiobjective genetic algorithm: NSGA-II. *IEEE Transactions on Evolutionary Computation* 6: 182–97.

Derringer, G. C. 1994. A balancing act: Optimizing a product's properties. *Quality Progress* 27: 51–8.

Dey, S., Sultana, N., Kaiser, M. S., Dey, P. and Datta, S. 2016. Computational intelligence based design of age-hardenable aluminium alloys for different temperature regimes. *Materials and Design* 92: 522–34.

Duerig, T., Melton, K. N., Stockel, D. and Wayman, C. M. 1990. *Engineering Aspect of Shape Memory Alloys*. Boston: Butterworth-Heinemann.

Harrington, E. C., Jr. 1965. The desirability function. *Industrial Quality Control* 21: 494–98.

Hashin, Z. and Shtrikman, S. 1963. A variational approach to the theory of the elastic behaviour of multiphase materials. *Journal of Mechanics and Physics of Solids* 11: 127–40.

Lielens, G., Pirotte, P., Couniot, A., Dupret, F. and Keunings, R. 1998. Prediction of thermo-mechanical properties for compression moulded composites. *Composites Part A: Applied Science and Manufacturing* 29: 63–70.

Nandi, A. K., Deb, K., Ganguly, S. and Datta, S. 2012. Investigating the role of metallic fillers in particulate reinforced flexible mould material composites using evolutionary algorithms. *Applied Soft Computing* 12: 28–39.

Olden, J. D., Joy, M. K. and Death, R. G. 2004. An accurate comparison of methods for quantifying variable importance in artificial neural networks using simulated data. *Ecological Modelling* 178: 389–97.

Sinha, A., Sikdar (Dey), S., Chattopadhyay, P. P. and Datta, S. 2013. Optimization of mechanical property and shape recovery behavior of Ti-(~49 wt%) Ni alloy using artificial neural network and genetic algorithm. *Materials and Design* 46: 227–34.

Zitzler, E., Laumanns, M. and Thiele, L. 2001. *SPEA2: Improving the Strength Pareto Evolutionary Algorithm*. Technical Report 103. Computer Engineering and Networks Laboratory (TIK), Swiss Federal Institute of Technology (ETH) Zurich, Zurich, Switzerland.

9

Concluding Remarks

Different techniques of computational intelligence (CI) and their applications in the field of materials design were discussed in Chapters 4 through 8. Those chapters dealt with issues related to different aspects of materials design and how to approach them with available CI techniques. But certain points, which are not directly related to CI-based materials design but need special mention, are discussed in this chapter.

9.1 Conventional versus CI-Based Materials Design

CI-based materials modelling and optimisation and other informatics-based approaches differ significantly from conventional modelling approaches to materials design, which depend heavily on the analytical or numerical approaches of mathematics. In this situation a miscibility gap exists between the two approaches. Designers who espouse conventional modelling are of the opinion that the other approaches do not have the necessary scientific underpinnings, and those who support informatics or CI-based modelling highlight the limitations of the analytical models in practical applications. In an attempt to be unbiased, it can easily be said that both groups are partially correct. But the limitations in both types of modelling can be overcome by proper mixing approaches. There are several ways through which these two apparently parallel efforts of designing materials may benefit, but the approaches have to be from both sides. CI-based materials designers are in a better position in this regard, as

1. They can find the areas where *ab initio* or other science-based analytical or numerical approaches may be incorporated in the area of practical materials design, to make the solutions more reliable and robust.

2. They can find the areas of analytical or numerical modelling where CI techniques could be employed to overcome unnecessary assumptions or simplifications. This type of activity has already started to some extent, in the form of fuzzy–finite element, fuzzy–cellular automata or fuzzy–Monte Carlo.

On the other hand, the conventional modelling group can identify the shortcomings of its approaches and techniques and seek solutions in the area of informatics or CI tools. Perhaps in some areas this type of amalgamation could create magic. Computational facility has not stopped improving. Thus researchers trying to develop improved materials from materials modelling, simulation and optimisation shall acquire greater ease in computing their requirements, and will generate more and more effective solutions for developing improved materials. In the age of computational design, the two approaches should come together in a synergistic approach towards improving the quality of materials to meet society's needs.

9.2 Microstructure

Microstructures of materials, including fractographs, obtained via light or electron microscopy are one of the most important means of characterising materials. Irrespective of the type of microscope, unlike in previous practices, today microstructure information is collected as digital images. The quantification of microstructure can be used for correlation with its properties. Several image processing types of software are being supplied with the microscopes, particularly the optical ones, which can analyse the microstructure including grain size measurement, phase fraction calculation and so forth. This is done using computational steps depending on the rudimentary tools of digital image processing. These types of software differentiate the phases based on a greyscale. Phases having the same grey level but different shapes of grain cannot be differentiated. Those with the same grey level but with differences in morphology are not separated. Phase separation using a greyscale becomes difficult for multiphase microstructures. This is expected, as materials engineers are rarely involved in image processing or analysis of microstructure. Numerous research activities are occurring in the field of image processing by computer engineers who are trying to solve other image-related problems. Most of the research is in the field of defense or other type of security. Significant work is also taking place in the field of medical imaging. Microstructures can also provide huge challenges for image processing/analysis researchers, but this area is generally neglected. CI techniques can play a significant role in solving the problems of quantification, classification or clustering of microstructures, as they are already doing for images from other fields, such as recognition of alphabets in different languages, recognition of characters from hand-written manuscripts and so forth (Soille 2004). This particular area has not been considered in this book because of the absence of adequate work.

9.3 Green Design

Two important aspects are sometimes neglected during the design of any product including materials. The first is the cost of the product to make it competitive in the market, and the second is consideration of the environment. Any material being developed can have an impact on the environment in any part or even the whole of its product life cycle, that is, from the extraction of raw materials to final disposal. There may be some relation between the cost of the material and its environmental impact (OTA Report 1992). For example, recycling of the material, reducing toxic content, government encouragement for recycled products and environmental labelling can have a positive impact on cost reduction. There are other design issues which can effectively reduce the cost of the product, such as reducing the weight of the product and increasing its durability.

In the case of materials design all of the aforementioned factors may be taken into consideration. Recycling is a major issue, particularly for polymeric materials. Designing recyclable polymers or suitable products for which recycled polymers could be safely used are major concerns for materials engineers. Designing less expensive biodegradable polymers is another challenge. Reducing the weight of any product, such as machine parts, leads to a lower consumption of materials, causing less disturbance to the environment. Replacing plain carbon steel by high-strength steel reduces the cost of the material because a lower amount of steel is required; this has been shown by several researchers. In the case of designing automobiles, reduction of weight through proper design and selection of materials reduces fuel consumption and thus can have a direct impact on the environment. Proper disposal of scrap electronic materials is an issue materials engineers need to solve. The most important issue in the design of green materials is the development of extraction/synthesis and other processing methods that emit less pollution. These aspects are generally neglected during the design process but need to be handled with more care during this phase. How CI could be utilised for this purpose needs to be explored.

9.4 Handling Uncertainty

Uncertainty is another issue materials engineers occasionally face. Uncertainty can be defined as doubt or vagueness, or something not definitely known. It can occur in the behaviour of the constituents of the materials and in the influence of the process parameters on the final performance of the materials. Thus uncertainty influences decisions and designs in engineering. Reducing uncertainty is a difficult proposition in the case of complex materials systems. The simplistic approach is to replace uncertainty with deterministic approaches, but as a result an infeasible solution will be reached. The other approach is learning to handle uncertainty through adoption of a proper method.

In science uncertainty mostly means measurement uncertainty and is tackled through error analysis. Werner Heisenberg introduced in 1927 the uncertainty principle, which asserts that it is impossible to determine simultaneously with unlimited precision the position and movement of a particle. In the field of engineering there is uncertainty in almost every area of research. In the case of designing controls for dynamical systems, uncertainty means the difference between models and reality. This is practical uncertainty. But in the case of engineering there exists theoretical uncertainty in the form of vagueness, which has been considered in the discussion on fuzzy logic. The risk of engineering design depends on the uncertainty of attaining the objective. This may have its root in uncertainty due to design imprecision and probabilistic uncertainty due to noise. Computational design depends solely on the certainty of the model predictions. It leads to model uncertainty, where certainty of a model is nothing but the accuracy of a mathematical model to describe the physical system (Thunnissen 2003). There is another issue called design uncertainty, which describes the variables which the designer does not know how to handle. All of these are part of any practical engineering design process, including materials design. It needs to be understood that the uncertainty issue will be there and the designer has to take that into account. For such cases modelling with CI techniques is definitely a better proposition, as these tools have the inherent capacity to handle uncertainty. The issues of imprecision and uncertainty in materials systems have been mentioned in Chapters 1, 4, 5 and 6. Here they are mentioned separately to emphasise the issues for materials designers.

9.5 Robust Solution

For all practical purpose the computationally generated solutions need to be robust, but the measure of robustness of the solution is to some extent related to uncertainty. Robust solutions are those which are less sensitive to small changes in the predictor or input variables. In the case of designing materials finding robust solutions has immense importance. The final performance of materials depends on the composition, processing and microstructure. If the solution is such that small variations in these variables result in a large variation in the material's properties, then it would be difficult to convert such designed material into development. During the course of development or synthesis, a certain amount of variation in the actual designed inputs is

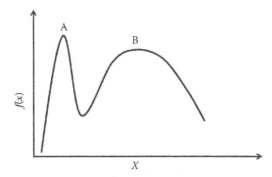

FIGURE 9.1
Global versus robust solutions.

unavoidable, particularly during large-scale industrial production. Thus in the selection of solutions it has to be checked whether the optimal solution is sensitive to variable perturbation in its vicinity. If the sensitivity is high then the optimal solution is not the robust solution (Deb and Gupta 2005). In the case of a maximisation problem shown in Figure 9.1, solution B is considered robust, though A is the optimal one.

9.6 DIKUW Hierarchy

In this book applications of several tools are discussed which deal with databases and extract knowledge from them. Knowledge management is an important issue today. In the case of materials informatics–based design using CI techniques is of course knowledge management. Russell Ackoff classified the content of the human mind into five categories (Ackoff 1989). The first one is data, which are raw and do not have any significance. The next level is information, where the data are processed to develop some relational connection to make them meaningful to some extent. Knowledge is the appropriate collection of information, to make it useful. Understanding is a cognitive and analytical process. Having understanding one can synthesise new knowledge from previous knowledge. The next level is wisdom, which provides the ability to judge right and wrong, good and bad. The hierarchy of data–information–knowledge–understanding–wisdom (DIKUW) is shown in Figure 9.2.

This issue is important for all the researchers in the handling of data. In the case of CI-based data-driven modelling it is easily possible to develop the relations and convert the data to information. The relations can provide the inherent pattern within the system. It can be extracted in the form of sensitivity analyses for artificial neural network models or if–then rules in

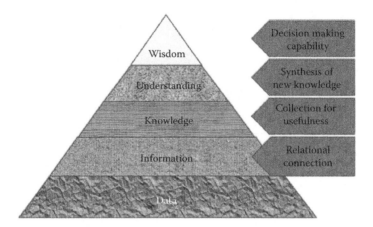

FIGURE 9.2
DIKUW hierarchy.

the case of fuzzy or rough set modeling. This provides the knowledge about the system. But the final understanding and wisdom may not be provided by the computational tools. People working with artificial intelligence (AI) claim that AI reaches the understanding level, as it can synthesise knowledge from previous knowledge. Whether the claim is true or not, it needs to be remembered that assimilating the knowledge to develop understanding of a system is an effort in which the researcher should have active participation. Without achieving understanding of a system wisdom is not achieved. An expert system in AI has the capability to make decisions, but expert knowledge needs to be supplied to make it work. The knowledge may come from data; but without human input in the domain of knowledge or wisdom, a good expert system is difficult to build. As the tools dealt with in this book are part of AI and also called computational intelligence, users should not become biased regarding the capability of the tools. Researchers should use checks in every point to compare their findings with those of materials science and engineering. The science, the acquired wisdom of civilisation, should not go to the back seat for even a moment.

References

Ackoff, R. L. 1989. From data to wisdom. *Journal of Applied Systems Analysis* 16: 3–9.
Deb, K., and Gupta, H. 2005. *Searching for Robust Pareto-Optimal Solutions in Multi-objective Optimization*. Evolutionary Multi-Criterion Optimization. Lecture Notes in Computer Science 3410, pp. 150–64. New York: Springer Science+Business Media.

OTA Project Staff Report. 1992. *Green Products by Design: Choices for a Cleaner Environment*. Office of Technology Assessment. Retrieved from: https://www .princeton.edu/~ota/disk1/1992/9221/922101.PDF (accessed 20 March 2016).

Soille, P. 2004. *Morphological Image Analysis–Principles and Applications*. Berlin: Springer-Verlag.

Thunnissen, D. P. 2003. Uncertainty classification for the design and development of Complex Systems. In *3rd Annual Predictive Methods Conference*, 16–17 June 2003, Newport Beach, CA.

Index

Note: Page numbers in italics refer to figures.